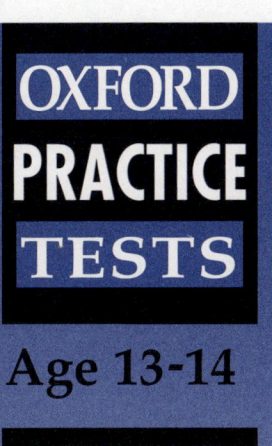

OXFORD
PRACTICE
TESTS

Age 13-14

MATHEMATICS

Practice Tests

for Key Stage 3

MATHEMATICS

Angela Royston and John Aldridge

OXFORD

OXFORD
UNIVERSITY PRESS

Great Clarendon Street, Oxford OX2 6DP

Oxford University Press is a department of the University of Oxford.
It furthers the University's objective of excellence in research, scholarship,
and education by publishing worldwide in

Oxford New York

Athens Auckland Bangkok Bogotá Buenos Aires Calcutta
Cape Town Chennai Dar es Salaam Delhi Florence Hong Kong Istanbul
Karachi Kuala Lumpur Madrid Melbourne Mexico City Mumbai
Nairobi Paris São Paulo Singapore Taipei Tokyo Toronto Warsaw

with associated companies in Berlin Ibadan

Oxford is a registered trade mark of Oxford University Press
in the UK and in certain other countries

About the authors
Angela Royston is a professional writer, who is author – at the last count – of over 100
educational books. She lives in North London with her two teenage children; John Aldridge
has over twenty years experience of developing educational assessment materials.

Acknowledgements
Robert Fell of Wood Green High School, Wednesbury for editorial work.

First published 1999

ISBN 0 19 838249 9

Packaged by Aldridge Press
Designed by Geoffrey Wadsley
Edited by Angela Royston
Illustrations by John and Jane Booth
Typeset in Garth Graphic
Printed in Hong Kong

Contents

It has been shown that practising for National Tests (SATs) improves a student's scores. This book provides:

1   practice tests for Mathematics National Tests at Key Stage 3 for levels 4 to 7
2   a method of assessing the level you are currently working at.

The average student is expected to gain level 5, while the majority (about 75 percent) will gain level 4, 5 or 6. A further 10 percent will gain level 7.

Tiers and levels in SATs

The National Test papers are arranged in tiers and are designed to cover a range of abilities. Your teacher will decide which tier you will sit: Level 3-5, Level 4-6, Level 5-7 or Level 6-8. Each tier consists of two one-hour written papers and a mental arithmetic test. In each tier the questions at the lowest level come first and the hardest level last. To reach the highest level in your tier, you have to finish the paper. If you do not finish the paper, do not worry – you can still reach one of the lower levels covered by the paper.

Test practice papers

This book contains ten practice tests. Troublespots Tests 1 and 6 give extra practice and help in topics which students commonly find difficult. Use the *Hints* to solve the questions.

There are two tests at each of level 4, level 5, level 6 and level 7. By covering only one level in each of these papers, you will get a better idea of how well you can do at any level and which topics you are weak in. The first of each pair of tests is slightly easier than the second test. Read 'Marking the tests' before trying the second test at any level.

Practising skills

In the National Tests the questions are often put into a situation you may be unfamiliar with. Don't panic! Read the question carefully and think through the question – you may well be able to answer it. The tests in this book provide practice in the skills you will need. The questions in the National Tests will provide opportunities for you to show those skills.

Calculator symbol

One paper in the National Tests allows the use of a calculator, and the other does not. In this book the calculator symbol beside a question shows that you can use a calculator. It is important to practise skills without using a calculator, so look for the symbol before using one.

Before you start a test

1   Make sure you have a quiet place to work where you will not be disturbed.
2   Have some spare paper beside you in case you need more space for your working out.

Time allowed for each test

Give yourself 30 minutes for each test. If at the end of 30 minutes you have not completed the test, make a note of where you got to and carry on with the rest of the test. When you assess your level only count the marks you scored during the first half hour.

Marking the tests

Use the answer pages to mark each test. Mark each question carefully and think about where you went wrong. If you get a question wrong, check whether you know how to tackle the topic but just made a careless mistake or whether you need to do more work on the topic. The title of the question tells you what topic to ask for more help with or more work on. If you scored:

Less than 50% – You still have a lot of work to do at this level.

50–70% – Pick out the topics you are having difficulty with and do more work on them.

70% or more – Well done, you will most likely pass at this level. Now try the next level.

If you get less than 70% in the first test at a level, do some more work before attempting the second test. When starting a new level, do not expect necessarily to pass it first time. This book helps you to improve and practise your skills so that you will do better next time.

• Formulae •

These formulae will be printed on the National Test papers.

AREA	LENGTH

Circle

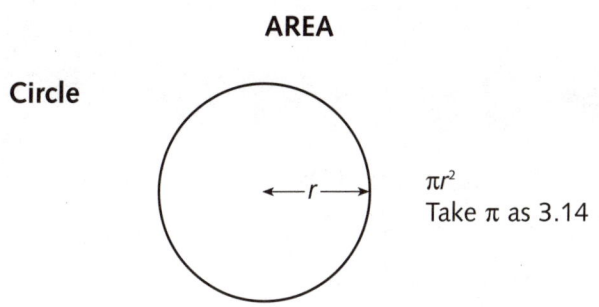

πr^2
Take π as 3.14

Circle

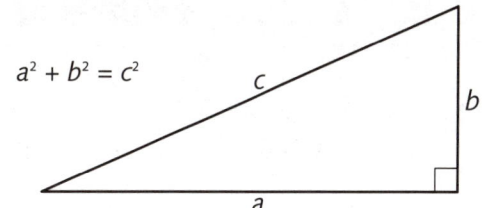

circumference $= 2\pi r$

Triangle

$$\frac{\text{base} \times \text{height}}{2}$$

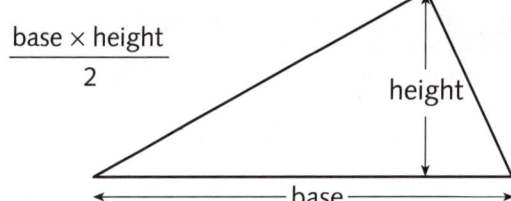

For a right-angled triangle

$a^2 + b^2 = c^2$

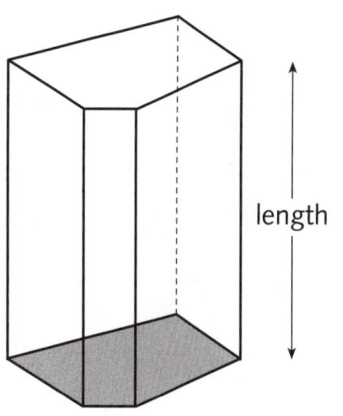

Parallelogram

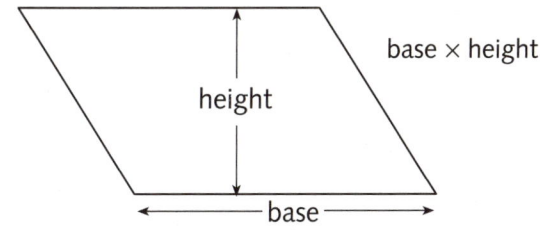

base $\times$ height

VOLUME

Prism

Trapezium

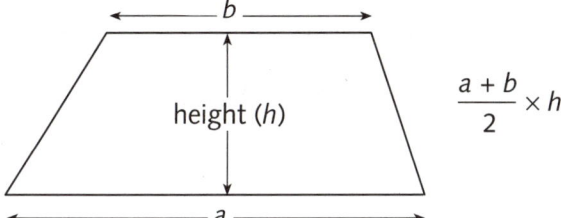

$$\frac{a + b}{2} \times h$$

area of cross-section $\times$ length

• **Test 1** with *Hints* •	Time started	:
	Time finished	:

Decimals

1 Darren has these cards:

| 4 | 7 | 1 | 5 | 0 | . | 2 |

a What is the smallest number he can make using three of the cards?

☐ ☐ ☐

Hint Should you put the numbers before or after the decimal point?

b Darren puts down 5 then 0. How should he lay down the rest of the cards to make the largest possible number between 1000 and 10,000?

| 5 | 0 | ☐ | ☐ | ☐ | ☐ |

Hint How many numbers before the decimal point?

c Darren puts down 7 2 5 4. Add one card to make a number that is 100 times smaller than 7254. You can add the card anywhere.

☐ ☐ ☐ ☐ ☐

Hint Think about the decimal point.

Decimals, fractions, percentages

2 Fill in the chart to show which decimals, simple fractions and percentages are equal to each other:

	Decimal	Fraction	Percentage
	0.1	$\frac{1}{10}$	10%
a	0.2	$\frac{1}{5}$	
b		$\frac{1}{4}$	25%
c			30%
d		$\frac{2}{5}$	
e	0.6		
f	0.75		
g	0.9		90%

Hint A percentage is the top line of a fraction over 100.

PAGE TOTAL

Percentages

3

a   In a test, Sophia scores 24 out of 60. What percentage is this?

_____

b   In the same test, Henry scored 25%. What mark out of 60 did he get?

_____

More percentages

4   A tray of peaches has these two stickers on it.

a   How much does each of these peaches cost?

_____

Hint You are buying 6 peaches for £1.20.

b   How much does each peach usually cost?

_____

c   One of the peaches is damaged so the shop manager reduces the price by 10%. By how much is the price reduced?

_____

d   The following week, the price of £1.20 is increased by 25%. By how much does the price rise?

_____

Calculating with negative numbers

5   Work out the value of the following:

a $3 - {}^-6 + {}^-5 - 4 =$ _____

b $-12 + {}^-8 - 1 + 2 =$ _____

c $12 - (-4) - 6 =$ _____

d $6 \times (-2) =$ _____   **e** $-4 \times -8 =$ _____

f $25 \div (-5) =$ _____   **g** $-36 \div -4 =$ _____

h $-(-6 + 11) =$ _____   **i** $-36 \div 6 =$ _____

Hint $-(-a) = +a$;   minus × minus = plus;   minus ÷ minus = plus

PAGE
TOTAL

Metric and imperial units

6 Isabel decides to measure her weight and height. Read the scales and write in the amount:

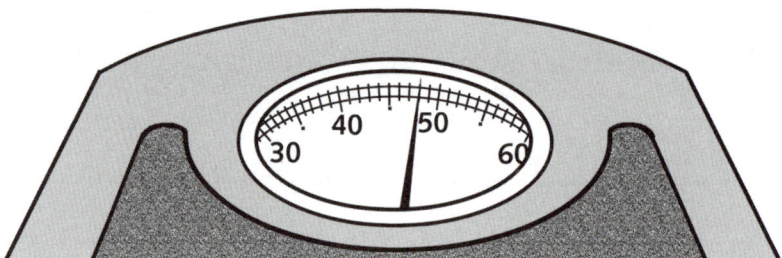

a   Weight _____ kg

   Hint First work out what each division on the weighing scale represents.

Isabel wants to know her weight in imperial units.

> 1 kg = 2.2 lb   14 lb = 1 stone

b   Convert Isabel's weight to the nearest lb.

_____

   Hint Will there be more lbs than kg or less? If more, then multiply; if less, divide.

c   What is her weight in stones and pounds?

_____

   Hint Will there be more stones or less?

Probability

7 Suppose you spin two coins to see whether each falls heads or tails.

a   Using H for heads and T for tails, list all the possible pairs of outcomes:

_____

   Hint To be sure you have all the possible outcomes, imagine two different coins, e.g. a 10p and a 5p.

b   Use the list to find the probability that you will throw two heads.

_____

c   What is the probability you will throw a head and a tail? _____

PAGE TOTAL

Drawing angles accurately

8 Andrew worked out that a pie chart should have the following angles:

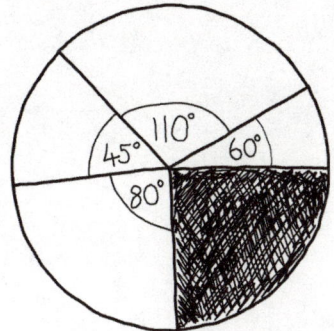

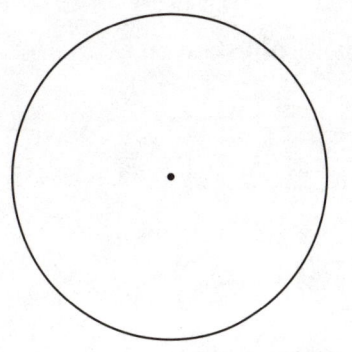

Make an accurate drawing of the pie chart.

Hint Make sure that you place the point of the angle indicator on your protractor at the centre of the circle.

Shade the last sector and measure its angle: _____

Accurate drawing

9 Lindsey designed a house for her hamster and made this rough sketch.

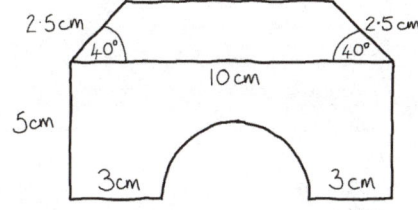

Make an accurate drawing of her sketch.

PAGE TOTAL

• **Test 2** •	Time started	:
	Time finished	:

Number

1 Fill in the blank spaces in the boxes so that each box is equal to 24:

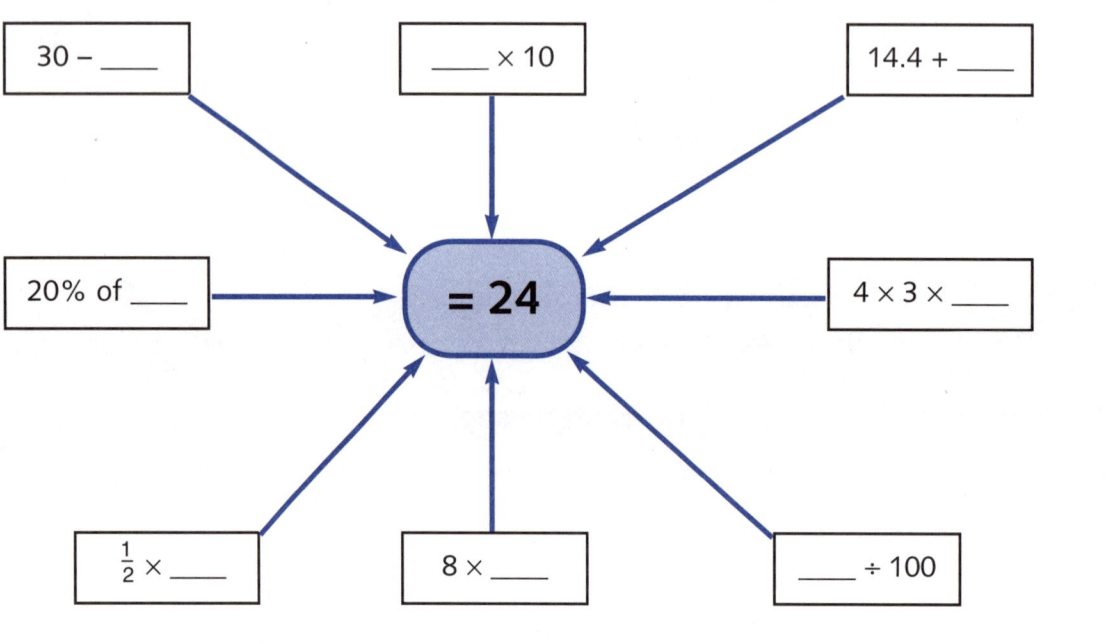

Number patterns

2 Fill in the blanks in the following number lines:

a   −5   −3   ___   1   3   5   7   ___   11

b   1.83   1.85   1.87   ___   1.91   1.93   ___   1.97   1.99

c   2.4   2.0   1.6   ___   0.8   0.4   0   ___   −0.8

Find three different ways of continuing the following sequence:

d   1   4   ___   ___

The rule is _____

e   1   4   ___   ___

The rule is _____

f   1   4   ___   ___

The rule is _____

PAGE TOTAL

Money calculations

3 Abi has £30 to spend. She wants to buy

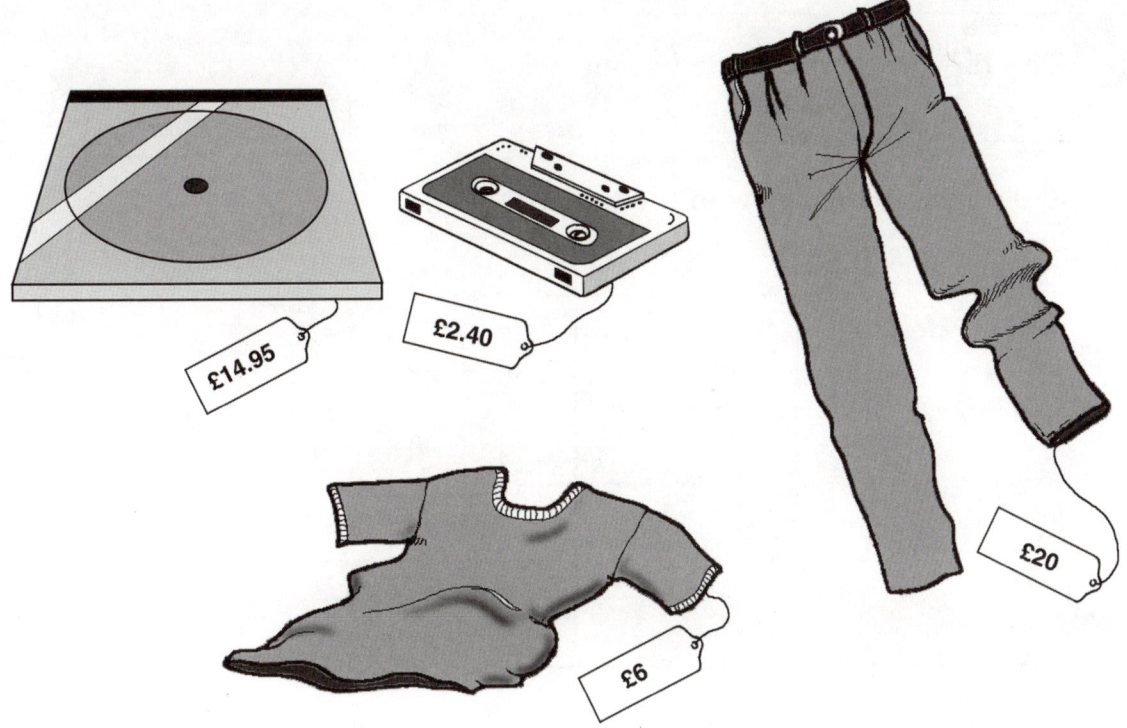

£14.95   £2.40   £20   £6

a   What is the price of the CD to the nearest £? _____

b   What is the price of the audio tape to the nearest £? _____

c   Can Abi buy all the items she wants for £30? _____

d   Which items should she buy to spend as much of her money as possible?

_____

When Abi goes back a few days later the shop is having a sale.
The T-shirt is now half-price.

Half Price Sale

e   What does it cost now? _____

f   By what percentage has the T-shirt been reduced? _____

The jeans have been reduced by 20%.

g   How much do the jeans cost now? _____

h   What fraction is 20%? _____

PAGE TOTAL

Measurement and shape

4   **a**   Calculate the perimeter of the rectangle.

_____

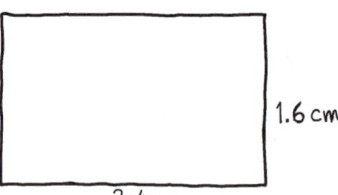

1.6 cm

2·4 cm

b   Find the area of the shaded shape below.

_____

c   Reflect the shape below in the line AB.

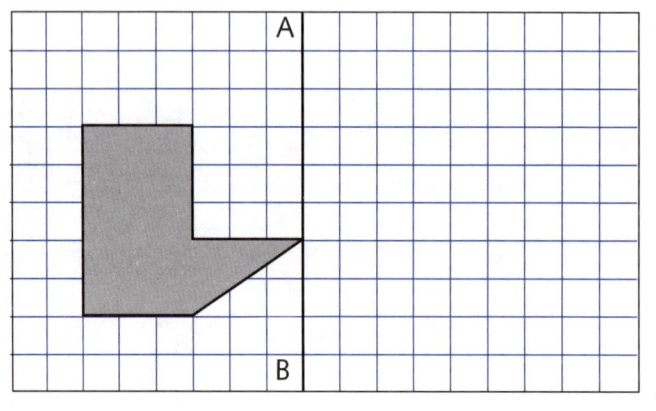

1 cm

Nets of 3-D shapes

5   **a**   Which of the nets shown below could be folded to make the box?

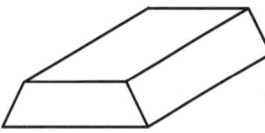

(a)

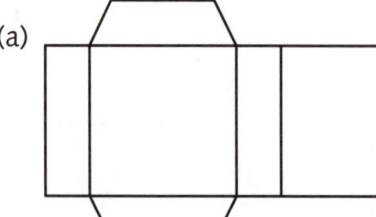

(b)

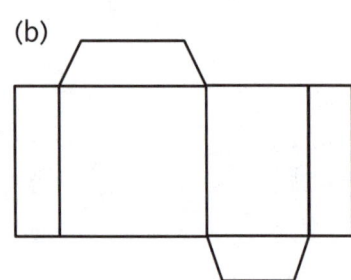

(c)

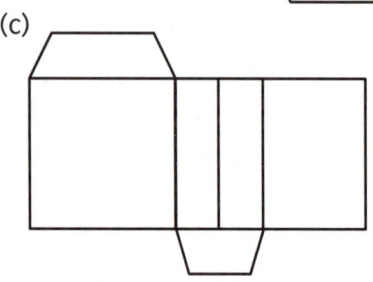

(d)

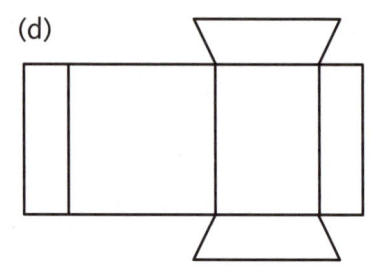

b   Draw a net for this solid:

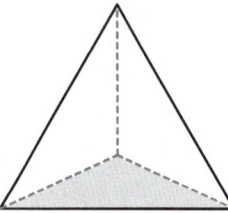

PAGE TOTAL

Mode, median, bar chart

6 A café sold the following items each day for a week:

	Mon	Tues	Wed	Thurs	Fri	Total
Flapjack	15	20	18	12	11	**76**
Crisps	35	30	22	45	18	___
Cheese roll	24	18	16	23	30	___

a   Complete the total column.

b   Which item was the most popular? _____

c   What is the median number of cheese rolls sold per day? _____

d   Draw a bar chart to show the number of flapjacks bought each day.

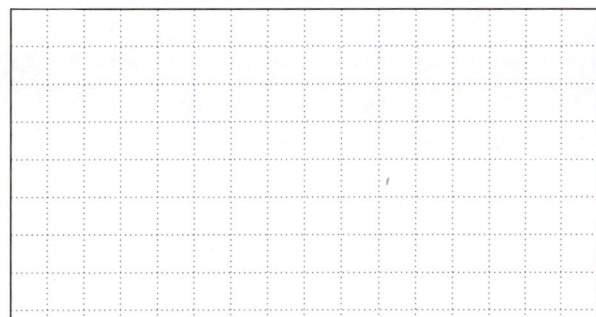

Probability

7 A survey of the colour of cars in a car park gave the following results:

	number of cars
white	2
red	9
blue	2
yellow	3
green	2

a   How many cars are there in the car park?

_____

b   Trina says that a car is more likely to be blue or white than yellow or green. Explain why she is wrong.

_____

c   What is the probability of a car being blue? _____

d   Which colour has a probability of $\frac{1}{6}$? _____   e   of $\frac{1}{2}$? _____

PAGE
TOTAL

• **Test 3** •	Time started [:]
	Time finished [:]

Number

1

a

63 × 10	

b

81 × 100	

c

8100 ÷ 10	

d

$\frac{63000}{100}$	

e

630 ÷ 10	

f

810 × 10	

Fill in the right half of each box so that it equals the left half. Which boxes equal each other?

_____

_____

Fractions and percentages

2 **Fill in the table to show the simple fractions, decimals and percentages which equal each other. The second line has been done for you.**

Simple fraction	Decimal	Percentage
	0.1	10%
$\frac{1}{4}$	0.25	25%
	0.4	40%
$\frac{1}{2}$		
	0.6	
	0.7	70%
$\frac{3}{4}$		
		80%

PAGE TOTAL

Money calculations

3

Carla buys four pencils and a birthday card.

a   **How much does she spend?** _____

b   **What change will she get from £2?** _____

Ben buys three felt-tip pens, an eraser, two birthday cards and a bottle of glue.

c   **How much does he spend?** _____

d   **What change does he get from £10?**_____

Mariam gets £1.25 change from £5.

e   **How much did she spend?** _____

f   **She bought a birthday card, a bottle of correction fluid and one other item. What was it?** _____

Sara buys twice as many felt-tip pens as Ben and half as many pencils as Carla.

g   **How many felt-tip pens does she buy?** _____

h   **How many pencils does she buy?** _____

PAGE TOTAL

Congruent shapes, perimeter and area

4

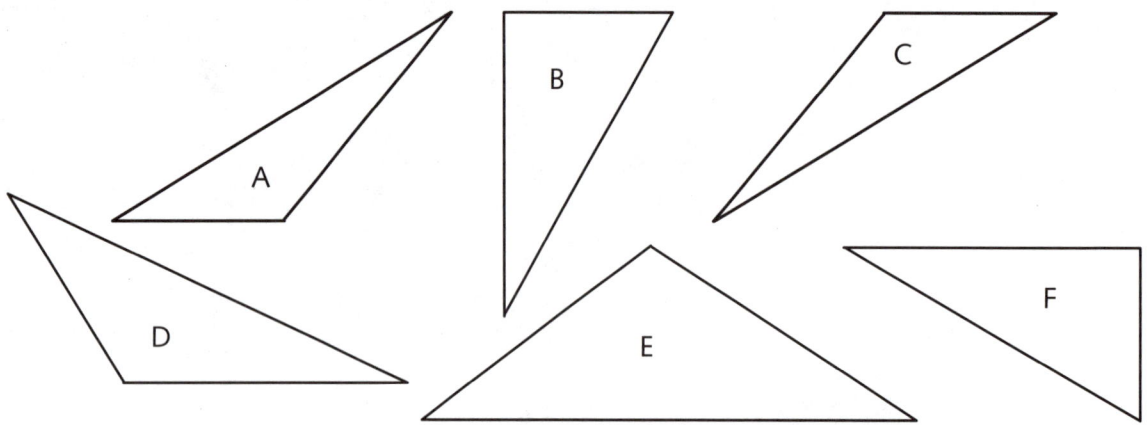

a   Which pairs of shapes are congruent?

_____

b   What is the perimeter of the shape below?

_____

c   What is the area of the shape?

_____

_____

42mm

55mm

56mm

37mm

Probability

5   Suppose you throw a 1 to 6 dice.

a   What is the probability that you throw a 3?

_____

b   What is the probability that you throw a number greater than 4? _____

c   What is the probability that you throw a number equal to or less than 4?

_____

d   What is the probability that you throw a number greater than 6? _____

e   What is the probability that you throw a number less than or equal to 6?

_____

PAGE TOTAL

Handling data

6

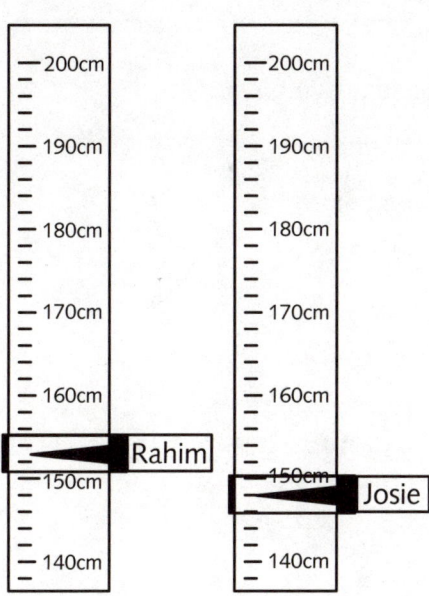

Rahim and Josie are in class 9XJ.

a   **What height is Rahim?** _____

b   **What height is Josie?** _____

These are the heights to the nearest centimetre of the rest of class 9XJ:

150 cm,   149 cm,   152 cm,   156 cm,   151 cm,

151 cm,   154 cm,   156 cm,   151 cm,   150 cm,

151 cm,   149 cm,   153 cm,   155 cm,   156 cm,

148 cm,   150 cm,   149 cm,   152 cm,   151 cm,

153 cm,   149 cm,   151 cm

c   **Fill in the tally chart below with the heights of *everyone* in class 9XJ:**

Height (cm)	Tally	Frequency
148–149		
150–151		
152–153		
154–155		
156–157		

d   **Which height group is the median?**

_____

e   **Which height group is the mode?**

_____

f   **Use the table to draw a frequency graph of the heights of students in the class 9XJ.**

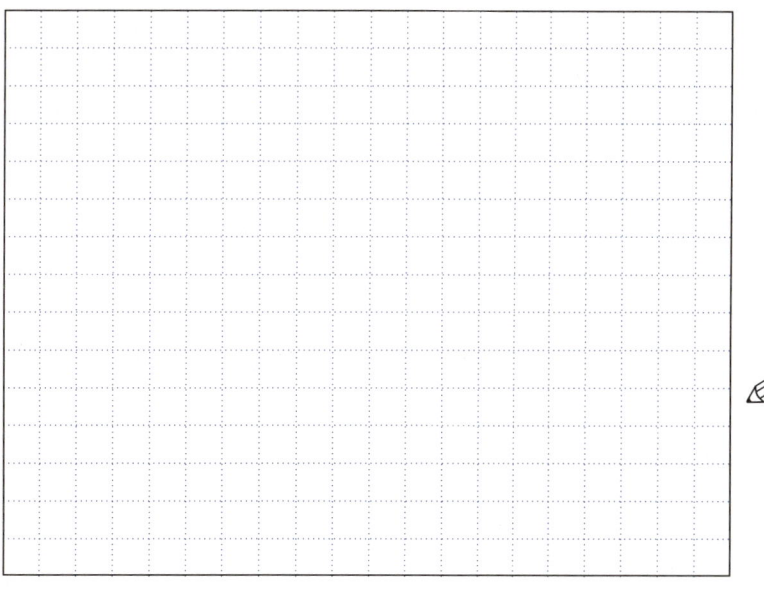

PAGE TOTAL

Time started	:
Test 4	
Time finished	:

Reading scales, range and mean

1 These are the thermometer readings taken on two consecutive days:

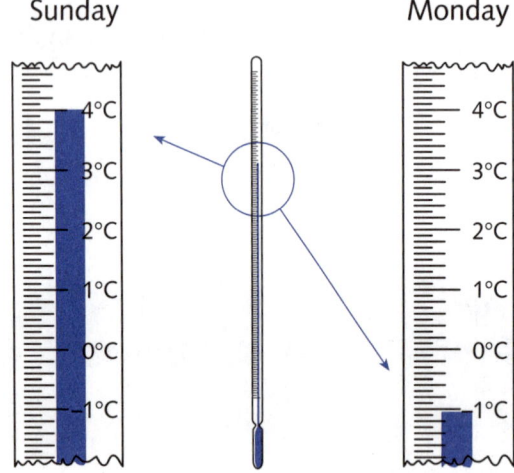

Sunday   Monday

a What was the temperature on Sunday? _____

b What was the temperature on Monday? _____

These are the temperatures measured in the shade on each of the other days for two weeks. Fill in the temperatures for Sunday and Monday:

	Sun	*Mon*	*Tues*	*Wed*	*Thurs*	*Fri*	*Sat*
Week 1	___	___	– 5°C	7°C	0°C	– 4°C	– 8°C
Week 2	3°C	6°C	10°C	9°C	2°C	– 2°C	0°C

c What is the range of temperature for week 2? _____

d What is the range of temperature for week 1? _____

e What is the mean temperature for week 2? _____

f What is the mean temperature for week 1? _____

g Using the mean and range, describe how the temperatures over the two weeks differed:

_____

_____

PAGE
TOTAL

Estimating calculations

2 Estimate an approximate answer to each of the following:

a 518×43 **b** 396×78 **c** 907×28 **d** 1905×409

   $\approx 500 \times 40$
   $\approx \mathbf{20000}$ $\approx$ _____ $\approx$ _____ $\approx$ _____

Work out the exact answer to each of the above multiplication sums on a piece of scrap paper.

   = _____   = _____   = _____   = _____

Estimate an approximate answer to each of the following:

e $359 \div 80$ **f** $1194 \div 32$ **g** $6741 \div 48$ **h** $8160 \div 75$

   $\approx$ _____ $\approx$ _____ $\approx$ _____ $\approx$ _____

Work out the exact answer to each of the above division sums on scrap paper.

   = _____   = _____   = _____   = _____

Formulae

3

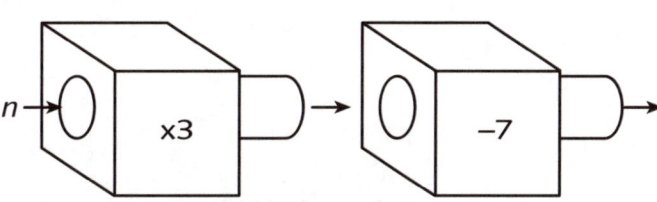

a   What is the output when $n = 8$? _____

b   What is the output when $n = -11$? _____

c   Write down the formula for the machine: _____

The monthly cost (T) of a mobile phone includes a fixed amount for line rental (r) and a varying amount depending on the number of minutes (m) the phone was used. The formula $T = r + 0.08m$ gives the monthly cost in £ when the charge per minute is 8p or £0.08.

d   Find T when $r = £30$ and $m = 100$ minutes.

   $T = £$ _____

e   Find T when the line rental is £25 per month and the phone is used for 80 minutes.

   $T = £$ _____

PAGE TOTAL

Co-ordinates

4

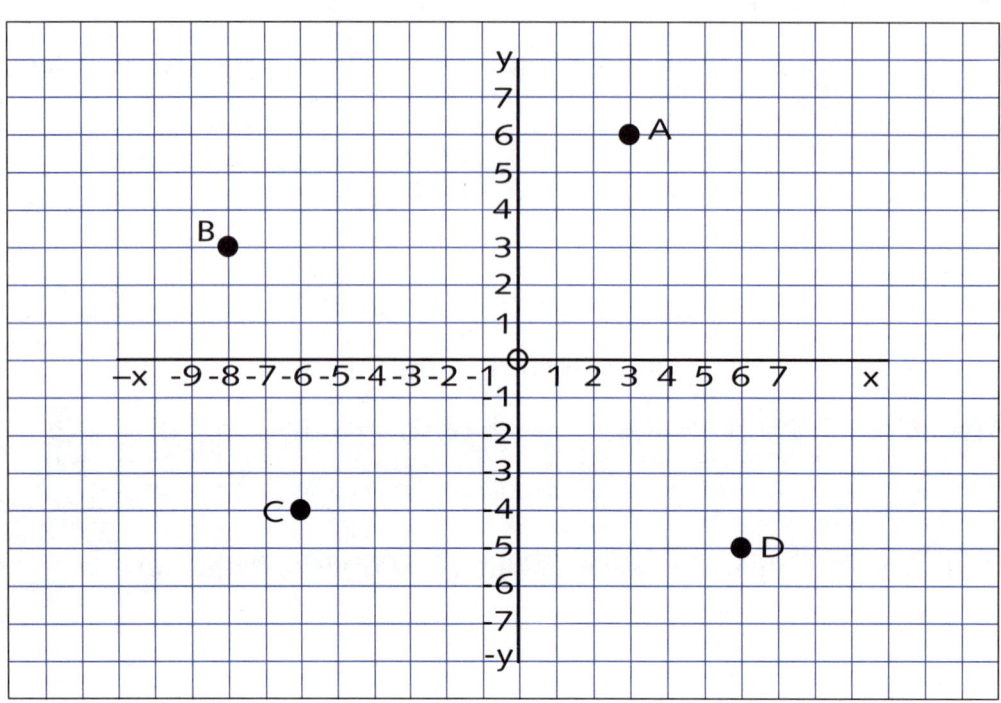

What are the co-ordinates of each of the points in the diagram?

a   A _____   b   B _____

c   C _____   d   D _____

e   **Mark in the following points on the diagram:**

  E (– 3, 6)

  F (– 6, 3)

  G (– 3, – 6)

  H (– 6, – 3)

  J (3, – 6)

f   **Which of the points could be joined to make a rectangle?** _____

g   **What is the perimeter of the rectangle?** _____

h   **What is the area of the rectangle?** _____

i   **Which three points are in a straight line?** _____

Metric and imperial units

5 Anna's shoe is 26.2 cm long. Trina's is 8 mm longer.

a   How long is Trina's shoe? _____ cm

b   Viraj's shoe is 14 mm longer than Anna's. How long is Viraj's shoe?

_____ mm

c   Use your calculator to find out the length of Anna's shoe in inches:

_____ inches

One inch is about 2.5 cm

d   Ben's shoe is 12.6 inches long. How many centimetres is it? _____ cm

Trina weighs 55 kilograms and Darren weighs 57.5 kilograms.

e   How many more grams does Darren weigh? _____ grams

f   How many pounds (lb) does Darren weigh?

_____ lb

One kilogram equals 2.2 lb

Pie charts

6 This pie chart shows the different ways class 9KO travel to school. There are 24 students in class 9KO and a third of them walk to school.

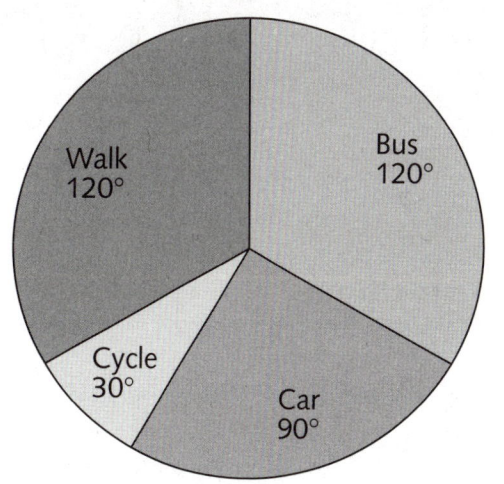

a   How many students walk? _____

b   How many of them travel by car? _____

c   How many students go by bus? _____

d   How many students cycle? _____

PAGE
TOTAL

Time started	:
Test 5	
Time finished	:

Multiplying and dividing by 10, 100, 1000

1 The flag shows what you must do to a number to get the next number.
Fill in the missing flags and numbers:

a 0.52 [× 10] → 5.2 [____] → 0.052 [____] → 52

b ____ [× 100] → 86 [____] → 0.086 [÷ 100] → ____

c 34 [____] → 0.34 [÷ 10] → ____ [____] → 340

Decimals and simple formulae

2  The Jones family hire a car for a week. They pay £22.40 a day plus 8p for every mile they travel. They make a note of the number of miles they travel each day.

	Sun	Mon	Tues	Wed	Thurs	Fri	Sat
Hire charge	£22.40	£22.40	£22.40	£22.40	£22.40	£22.40	£22.40
Miles/day	64.6	81.2	91.8	124.2	80.6	55.0	150.5
Mileage charge (to nearest p)							
Total charge							

a Fill in the table to find the cost of hiring the car on each day.

b What is the total cost of hiring the car for the week? _____

c Write a formula for calculating the daily cost. Use m to stand for the number of miles travelled.

_____

PAGE TOTAL

Algebra: solving simple equations

3   **Find the value of *n* in each of the following:**

a $3n = 12$ $n =$ _____   ☐

b $5n - 7 = 18$ $n =$ _____   ☐

c $2n = 5n - 15$ $n =$ _____.   ☐

d $-6 + 5n = 3n - 2$ $n =$ _____   ☐

Accurate drawing

4   **Make an accurate copy of this rough sketch:**

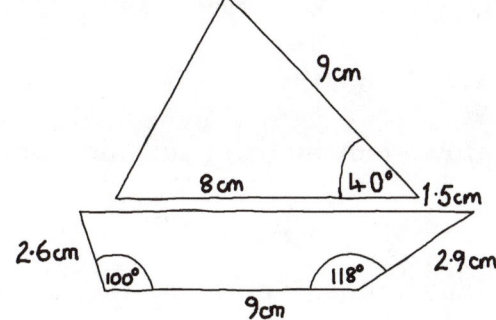

PAGE
TOTAL

Reading bar charts, range, mean

5 The following bar chart shows the hours of sunshine for each month of one year in the holiday resort of Sunshine City.

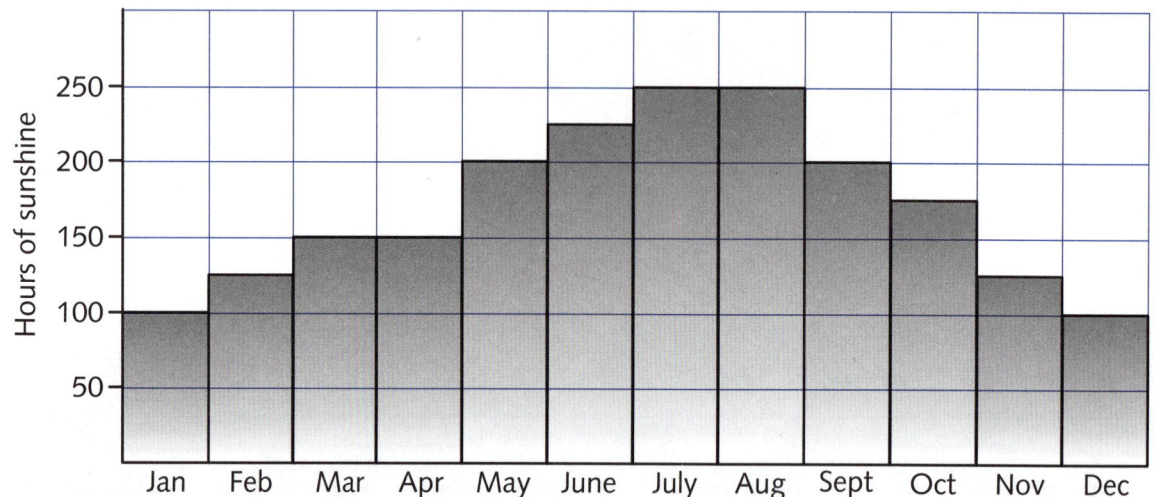

a   Which months had the most sunshine? _____

b   How many hours of sunshine were there in September?

_____ hours

c   Which other month had the same number of hours of sunshine?

_____

d   What was the range for the hours of sunshine? _____

e   What was the total number of hours of sunshine over the year? _____

f   What was the mean number of hours of sunshine per month? _____

Probability

6 Calculate the probability of picking each of the following cards from a well-shuffled pack of 52. Look at a pack of cards if you need to.

a   a black card _____

b   a heart _____

c   the ace of diamonds _____

d   a Jack, Queen or King _____

PAGE TOTAL

Rotational symmetry

7

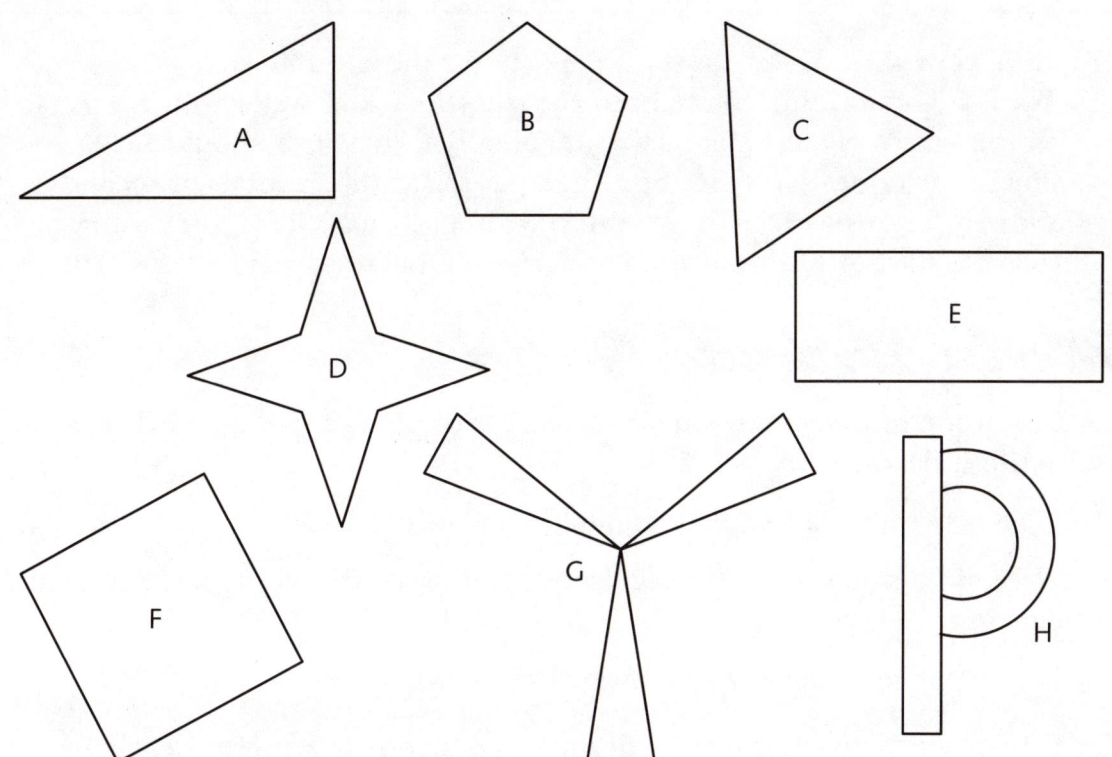

a   Which of the above shapes have rotational symmetry
of order 2 or higher? _____

b   Which shapes have rotational symmetry of order 3? _____

c   Which shapes have rotational symmetry of order 4? _____

d   Draw below a shape with rotational symmetry of order 1 only:

e   Which of these letters have rotational symmetry of order 2?

A B C D E F G H I J K L M N O P Q R S T U

V W X Y Z _____

PAGE
TOTAL

• Mental Arithmetic •

Time started

Time finished

1   Photocopy the answer sheet on page 28 for these tests.
2   Ask a friend or adult to read out the questions and write your answers on the answer sheet. The person reading the questions should read slowly each question twice and then pause for the number of seconds allowed for answering. Use a watch with a seconds timer. (Remember you can start to work out the answer while the question is being read.)

Mental Arithmetic Test A

For this group of questions you will have 5 seconds to work out each answer and write it down.

1   What is twenty-five point four multiplied by one hundred?

2   Write down a number with three digits that is bigger than thirty-five but smaller than thirty-five point five.

3   Look at the equation on your answer sheet. What is the value of m?

For this group of questions you will have 10 seconds to work out each answer and write it down.

4   If you buy a pen costing two pounds forty pence and a card costing eighty pence, how much change will you get from five pounds?

5   Look at the box of tins on your answer sheet. How many tins do three boxes hold?

6   Look at the bar chart on your answer paper. What is the total number of cats and dogs shown?

7   A secretary earned three hundred pounds per week. She was given a pay rise of five percent. How much extra does she earn now?

8   Multiply five by minus six.

9   Look at the diagram on your answer sheet. What size is angle B?

10   The length of each side of a square is five centimetres. What is the area of the square?

For this group of questions you will have 15 seconds to work out each answer and write it down.

11   Look at the net on your answer sheet. What shape is it for?

12   A watch shows the time to be five minutes past four. It is fifteen minutes fast. What is the correct time?

13   Look at the shapes on your answer sheet. Put a circle around the shape that is congruent to the shaded shape.

Mental Arithmetic Test B

Ask a friend or adult to read out the questions and write your answers on the answer sheet. The person reading the questions should read slowly each question twice and then pause for the number of seconds allowed for answering. Use a watch with a seconds timer. (Remember you can start to work out the answer while the question is being read.)

For this group of questions you will have 5 seconds to work out each answer and write it down.

1   What is fifty-six divided by seven?

2   How many grams are there in three kilograms?

3   Look at the angle on your answer sheet. What size is it in degrees?

For this group of questions you will have 10 seconds to work out each answer and write it down.

4   Look at the equation on your answer sheet. What is the value of p?

5   What is twenty-five percent of eighty?

6   Look at the spinners on the answer sheet. Circle the spinner which has a probability of one half of landing on black.

7   A tape costs six pounds ninety-nine pence. How much change do I get from ten pounds?

8   Look at the tally marks on your answer sheet. How many blue objects are shown?

9   Look at the two triangles on your answer sheet. How many of the small triangles would fit into the large one?

10   Look at the measurements on the answer sheet. Draw a ring around the smallest one.

For this group of questions you will have 15 seconds to work out each answer and write it down.

11   What is the next square number after sixty-four?

12   Imagine a round ball. If you made a straight cut through the ball, what would be the shape of the flat face made by the cut?

13   Look at the shape on the answer sheet. How many lines of symmetry does it have?

• Answer Sheet •

Mental Arithmetic Test A	*Mental Arithmetic Test B*

1   25.4

2

3   8 + *m* = 3

4   £2.40   80p   £5

5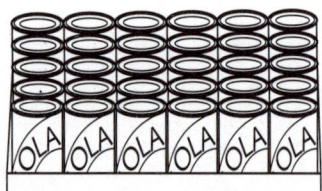

6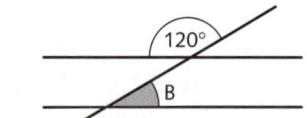

7   £300   5%

8

9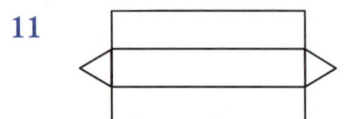

10

11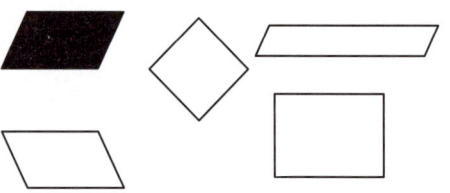

12   4.05   15 min

13

1

2

3

4   6*p* = 24

5   25%   80

6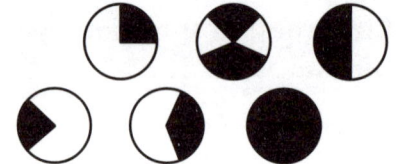

7   £6.99

8
Yellow   〰 ||
Blue   〰 〰 |||
Red   〰 〰 〰 |||

9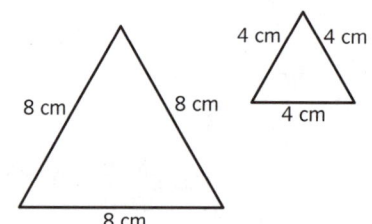

10   3.1 metres   86 cm
0.75 metres   210 cm

11

12

13

• **Mental Arithmetic** •	Time started	:
	Time finished	:

1   Photocopy the answer sheet for these tests on page 31.
2   Ask a friend or adult to read out the questions and write your answers on the answer sheet. The person reading the questions should read slowly each question twice and then pause for the number of seconds allowed for answering. Use a watch with a seconds timer. (Remember you can start to work out the answer while the question is being read.)

Mental Arithmetic Test C

For this group of questions you will have 5 seconds to work out each answer and write it down.

1   What is six point seven two divided by a hundred?

For this group of questions you will have 10 seconds to work out each answer and write it down.

2   Look at the shape on your answer sheet. Draw the shape after a rotation of ninety degrees clockwise.

3   What is eight point four minus three point nine?

4   Look at the equation on your answer sheet. What is the value of *m*?

5   Look at the diagram on your answer sheet. What is the size of the angle *x*?

6   A square has an area of sixty square metres. What is the area of a second square whose sides are half as long as those of the first square?

7   What is one eighth expressed as a decimal?

For this group of questions you will have 15 seconds to work out each answer and write it down.

8   A mobile phone costs three pounds a week rental and five pence a minute for local calls. I only use the phone for local calls and decide to spend a total of ten pounds a week. How long can I speak for?

9   Look at the numbers on your answer sheet. What is the mean of the numbers?

10   I leave for Spain on July the twenty-seventh and return home on the fifth of August. For how many nights am I away?

11   In a sale, a CD player is marked twenty-five percent off. It now costs sixty pounds. What did it cost originally?

12   The volume of a cube is one hundred and twenty-five cubic centimetres. What is the length of each side?

13   Look at the digits on your answer sheet. Arrange them to make the smallest possible number divisible by five. You must use all the numbers.

Mental Arithmetic Test D

Ask a friend or adult to read out the questions and write your answers on the answer sheet. The person reading the questions should read slowly each question twice and then pause for the number of seconds allowed for answering. Use a watch with a seconds timer. (Remember you can start to work out the answer while the question is being read.)

For this group of questions you will have 5 seconds to work out each answer and write it down.

1   Which is longer: fifty-six metres or nought point five six kilometres?

For this group of questions you will have 10 seconds to work out each answer and write it down.

2   Look at the right-angled triangle on your answer sheet. What is the length of the hypotenuse?

3   Three oranges cost ninety pence. How much will five oranges cost?

4   Look at the triangles on your answer sheet. Circle the two triangles which are congruent.

5   Tony has four blue ties, three red ties and a black tie. He takes a tie without looking. What is the probability that it is blue?

6   Write an approximate answer to the calculation shown on the sheet.

7   The mean of p, q and r is eight; p is twelve and q is five. What is r?

For this group of questions you will have 15 seconds to work out each answer and write it down.

8   Look at the formula on the answer sheet. If t equals four, what is the value of v?

9   Thirty percent of one pound eighty is fifty-four pence. What is thirty percent of ninety pence?

10   A plane travels two hundred and eighty kilometres in forty minutes. How far will it travel in an hour?

11   The probability that a horse will win a race is three-thirteenths. What is the probability that the horse will not win the race?

12   Look at the box on your answer sheet. What is the height of the box?

13   Look at the calculation on the answer sheet. Write down the answer.

• Answer Sheet •

Mental Arithmetic Test C	*Mental Arithmetic Test D*

Test C

1   6.72

2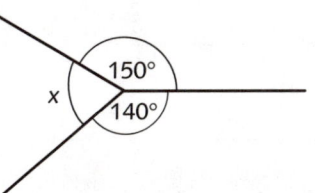

3   8.4   3.9

4   16 = 31 − 3m

5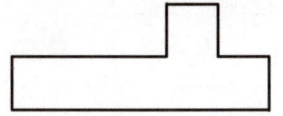

6   60 sq m

7 $\frac{1}{8}$

8   £3   5p   min

9   32   39   35   38

10   27 July   5 Aug

11   £60

12   125 cm³

13   6   1   5   3   9

Test D

1   56 m
       0.56 km

2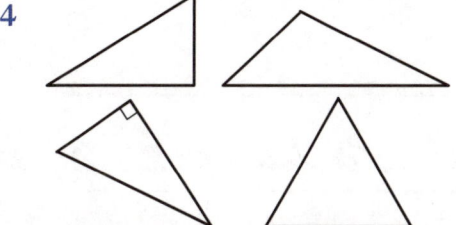

3   90p

4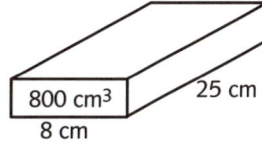

5   4 blue   3 red   1 black

6 $\dfrac{6.2 \times 1.8}{5.9}$

7   8
       $p = 12$ $q = 5$

8 $v = 6 + \dfrac{5t}{2}$ $v =$

9   30%   £1.80   54p

10   280 km

11 $\dfrac{3}{13}$

12

13   −5(6 − 18)

	Time started	:
• **Test 6** with *Hints* •	Time finished	:

Dividing by and square roots of fractions

1 Calculate the following without using a calculator:

a $8 \div \frac{1}{4} =$ _____

b $49 \div 0.7 =$ _____

c $\dfrac{3 \times 5}{\frac{1}{3}} =$ _____

d $\dfrac{16.24}{0.8} =$ _____

e $\sqrt{0.81} =$ _____

f $\sqrt{0.16} =$ _____

g $\sqrt{(\frac{1}{9})} =$ _____

h $\sqrt{(\frac{4}{25})} =$ _____

Calculating with square roots

2 The diagram shows the plan of an area designed for guinea pigs.

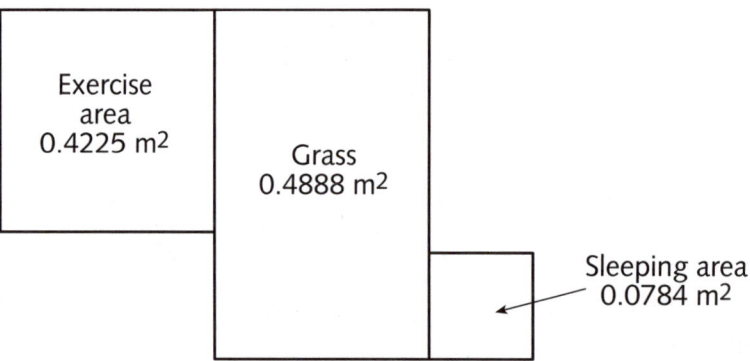

a If the sleeping area is square, what is the length of each side?

_____

Hint Use a calculator.

b If the exercise area is square, what is the length of each side?

_____

c The patch of grass is 0.94 metres long. What is the width?

_____

d What length of wire netting is required to go around the perimeter?

_____

PAGE TOTAL

Simplifying algebraic expressions

3   Simplify the following expressions:

a $5x + y - 2x - 2y =$ _____   ☐

b $2m - 3n - n + 3m =$ _____   ☐

c $6a + 4b - (2a - b) =$ _____   ☐

d $3s + 2(w - s) =$ _____   ☐

Algebraic equations

4   Jane, Dan, Shelly and Gareth each have a bag of marbles. The number of marbles in the bags are marked using *n* to stand for the same number each time.

a   **If Jane and Shelly put their bags together, write an expression for how many marbles they have in total:** _____   ☐

b   **If Dan and Gareth put their bags together, write an expression for how many marbles they have in total:** _____   ☐

c   Jane and Shelly now have the same number of marbles as Dan and Gareth, so they wrote:

   $(4n + 3) + (3n - 5) = (5n - 2) + (n + 8)$

   What is the value of *n*? _____   ☐

Proportion

5   If three cats cost £6.30 to feed a week, how much would 7 similar cats cost?

_____   ☐

Hint First work out how much one cat would cost.

PAGE TOTAL

Calculating speed and distance

6 **a** If a car travels 192 kilometres in 2.4 hours, how long will it take to travel

288 km? _____

Hint Find speed **or** work out how long it takes to travel 1 km.

b If a car travels at a steady speed of 84 km/hr, how long will it take to

travel 294 kilometres? _____

Hint First work out how long it takes to travel 1 km.

c If a motor bike travels 120 km in 1.6 hours, how far will it travel in 6

hours at the same speed? _____

Hint Find speed **or** work out how far it travels in 1 hour.

d If a 2.5 kg bag of grass seed covers 10 square metres of bare ground, how

much grass seed will be needed to cover 22 square metres? _____

Hint First work out how much grass seed covers 1 sq m.

Ratio

7 A paint tint is mixed from the basic colours red, blue, yellow and white in the ratio
1 : 5 : 4 : 2.

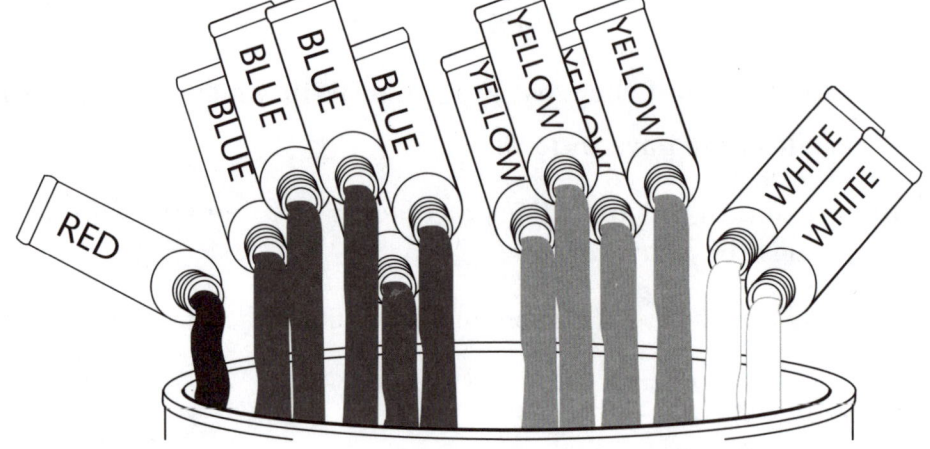

a The chemist puts 55 litres of blue into the machine. What quantity of
each other colour will he now need to add?

Red _____   Yellow _____   White _____

b What quantity of each colour will be needed to make 180 litres of paint?

_____

PAGE
TOTAL

Accurate drawing

8 Make an accurate drawing of this rough sketch for a model boat:

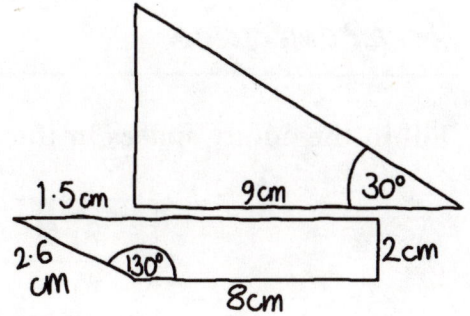

Probability

9 Complete this table showing all the possible outcomes of throwing two dice to help you answer the questions:

	First dice					
	1	**2**	**3**	**4**	**5**	**6**
1	1,1	2,1				
2		2,2				
3						
4						
5						
6						

Second dice

a   What is the probability of throwing two 4s? _____

b   What is the probability of throwing a 2 and a 4 on either dice? _____

c   What is the probability of throwing two numbers which add up to 9 or more? _____

PAGE TOTAL

Test 7

Time started [:]
Time finished [:]

Percentages

1 Fill in the empty spaces in the table. The first line has been done for you.

	Score	Total	Percentage
	30	80	37.5%
a		60	33.3%
b	12	30	
c	24		40%
d	18	72	
e	4.5	45	
f	32		80%
g	3		15%
h	25	40	

Finding the nth term in a sequence

2 **a** What is the next term in this sequence?

Sequence A: 4   7   10   13   16   _____

b Write down the formula for finding the nth term of sequence A.

_____

c What is the next term in this sequence?

Sequence B: 0   3   8   15   24   _____

d Write down the formula for the nth term of sequence B:

_____

e The formula for the nth term in a different sequence is $2n - 3$. Write out the first four terms:

_____   _____   _____   _____

PAGE TOTAL

Solving simple equations

3 Find the value of *x* in the following equations:

a   4*x* – 3 = 3*x* + 1 _____   **b**   8 – 5*x* = 2*x* – 13 _____

Ali and Carla both collect cards. Ali has 12 more than Carla.

c   If *a* = the number of cards Ali has and c = the number of cards Carla has, write an equation which describes the relationship between *a* and *c*.

_____

Ali gives 2 cards to Carla. He then has twice as many cards as her.

d   Write an equation which shows the relationship between Carla's

and Ali's cards now. _____

e   Solve your equations to find how many cards:

Ali started with _____ and Carla started with _____

Mapping

4   **a**   The table shows the values for the mapping *x* → 5*x* – 3. Complete the table:

x	*5x – 3*
1	2
2	
3	
4	
5	

b   Draw the next set of matches to show how this pattern continues:

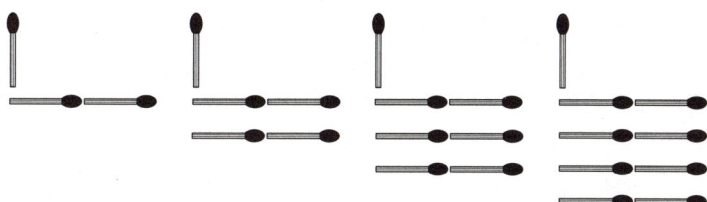

c   Give the rule for the *n*th term: _____

PAGE TOTAL

Calculating volume

5 The school secretary wants to order as many packets of coloured paper as she can fit into the top shelf of the store cupboard, allowing 10 cm space at the top of the cupboard.

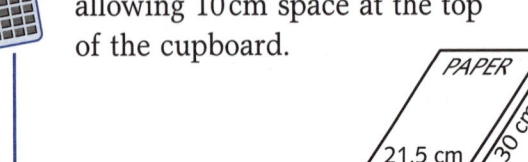

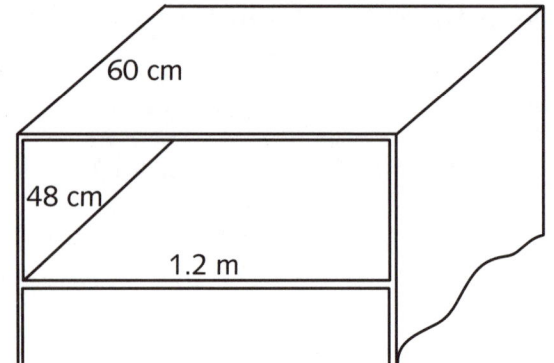

a   What is the volume of each packet? _____ cm³

b   What is the volume of the space available in the cupboard?

_____ cm³

c   How many packets can the cupboard hold? _____

Parallel lines and geometrical properties

6 In the diagram below, AB, DE and CF are parallel.

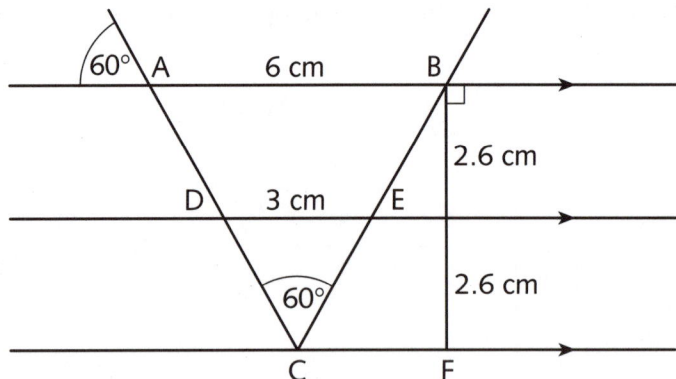

a   What size is angle CAB? _____

b   How do you know? _____

c   What size is angle ADE? _____

d   How do you know? _____

e   What kind of triangle is ABC? _____

f   What is the area of triangle ABC? _____

g   What kind of quadrilateral is ABED? _____

h   What is the area of ABED? _____

Frequency graphs, probability

7 Viraj counted the number of different coloured chocolate beans in a tube. Then he drew a graph:

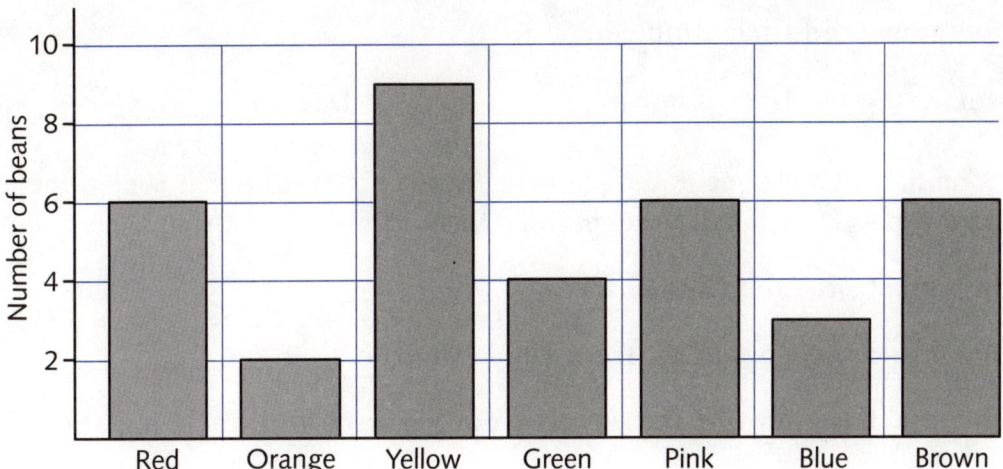

a How many beans are there in the tube? _____

b What percentage are yellow? _____

c What percentage are pink? _____

If Viraj picks a bean at random, what is the probability that it is

d blue? _____   **e** pink or red? _____

f neither brown nor orange? _____

If Viraj eats all the pink and red beans, what is the probability that the next bean he picks at random is

g brown? _____   **h** yellow or blue? _____

i Draw a pie chart to show the number of each colour of beans after Viraj eats all the red and pink ones. Fill in the table to help you.

	Number of beans	Angle in pie chart
Orange		
Yellow		
Green		
Blue		
Brown		

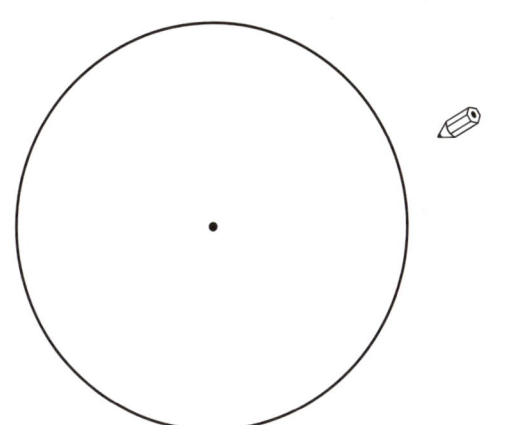

PAGE TOTAL

| • **Test 8** • | Time started | : |
| | Time finished | : |

Ratio

1 Aunt Maya sent £60 to be split between Alex, Sophie and Darren in the ratio 5 : 4 : 3.

a How much did each child get?

Alex _____   Sophie _____   Darren _____

Uncle Charlie sent a cheque to be split between the children so that Sophie got six times as much as Darren and Alex got three times as much as Darren. Alex got £9.

b How much was the cheque for? _____

c How much did Sophie get from Uncle Charlie? _____

d How much money did Darren get from his aunt and uncle together?

_____

e Which child got the most money altogether? _____

Using a calculator

2 Find the value of the following, correct to 2 decimal points:

a $\sqrt{20}$ = _____   **b** $6.74(52.8 + 301.14)$ = _____

c $\sqrt{2} + 5\sqrt{3}$ = ._____   **d** $5.2 + \sqrt{(13.42 - 6.12)}$ = _____

e Continue with this table to find the square root of 75 by trial and improvement, correct to 2 decimal places:

Guess	Result	Too high or too low?
8	64	too low
9	81	
8.5		

$\sqrt{75}$ = _____

PAGE TOTAL

Simplifying algebraic expressions

3 Simplify the following expressions:

a $2a + 3b + 3a - b =$ _____ ☐

b $3s + 4t - 2s + 3t - 6 =$ _____ ☐

c $3x - 6y + 2x + 4 - 5y =$ _____ ☐

Drawing lines on graphs

4

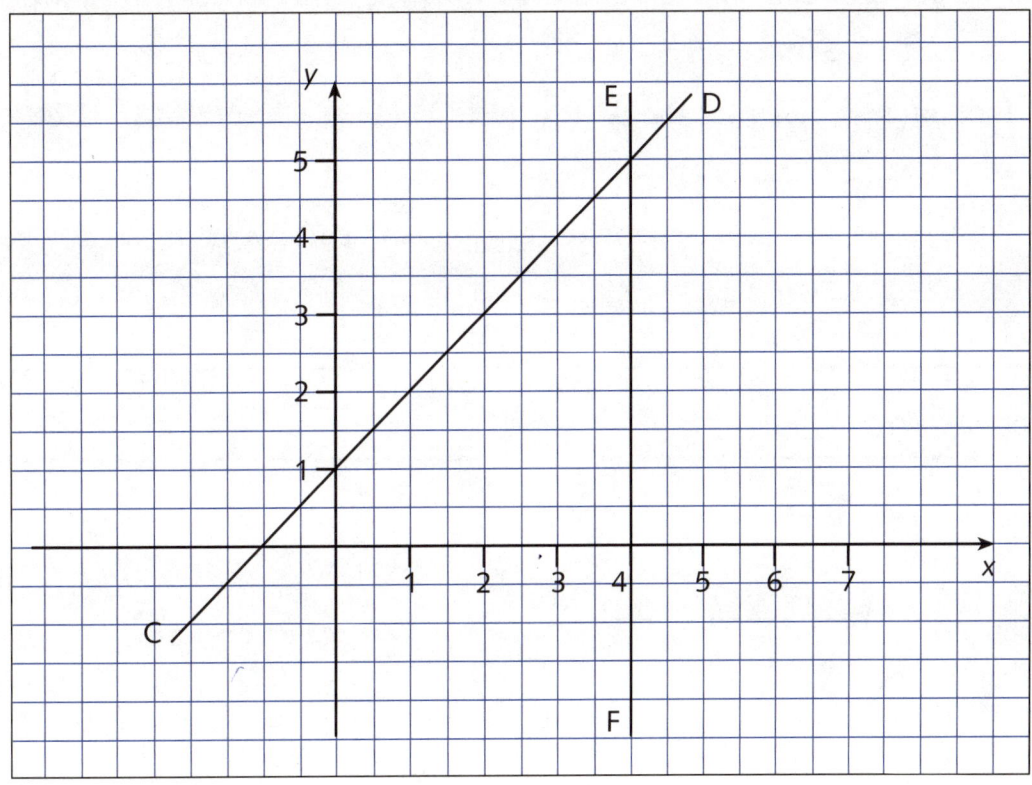

a Make a table of values and then draw the line AB whose equation is $2x + y = 4$.

x			
y			

b What is the point of intersection of the lines CD and EF? _____

c What is the point of intersection of the lines AB and CD? _____

d What is the equation of the line EF? _____

e Complete the equation for the line CD: $y = x +$ _____

PAGE TOTAL

Circumferance and area of a circle

5

In this old bicycle the front wheel has a diameter of 1.6 metres and the back wheel has a diameter of 20 cm.

a   What is the radius of the front wheel?

_____ cm

b   What is the circumference of the back wheel?

_____ cm

c   How far does the bicycle travel each time the front wheel turns once?

_____ cm

d   How many times does the back wheel turn for each turn of the front wheel? _____ cm

e   What is the area of a circle with the same dimensions as the front wheel?

_____ cm²

Bearings

6

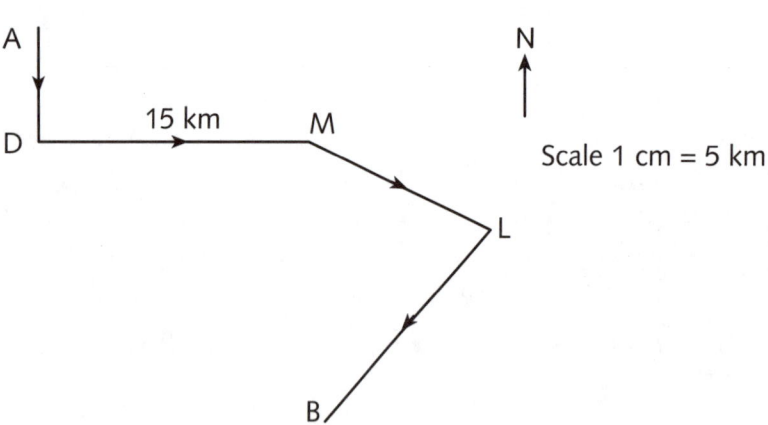

A

N

D | 15 km   M

Scale 1 cm = 5 km

L

B

The diagram shows the route a patrol helicopter took from the centre of the town A back to its base at B.

a   What bearing was it flying on between A and D? _____

b   Complete these instructions to tell the pilot to fly from D to M:

Fly for _____ km on a bearing of _____

c   Measure the bearing the pilot takes to get from M to L _____

d   Measure the bearing the pilot takes to get from L to B _____

PAGE TOTAL

Probability tossing two coins

7 Yasmin and Errol are playing a game which involves tossing two coins.

a   **Fill in the blanks in this table of all the possible outcomes:**

	First coin	
	H	T
Second coin H		
Second coin T		

They each have to throw two heads together to start the game.

b   **What is the probability that Yasmin throws two heads first time?** _____

c   **What is the probability that Errol throws a head and a tail?** _____

Scattergrams

8 Three groups in Class 9KR did scattergrams to see if there was any connection between: A) their height and their weight; B) the month of their birthday and how far they lived from school; C) how long they spent watching TV and how long they spent doing their homework last night. Their results are shown below.

(i)
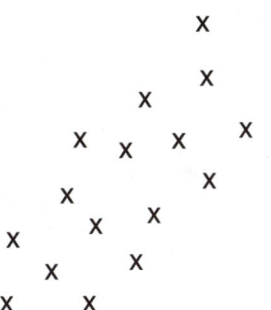

(ii)

(iii)
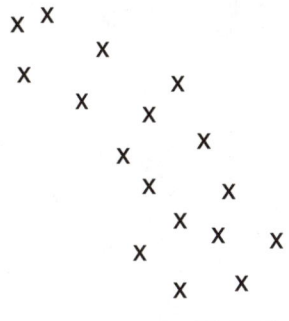

a   **Match the scattergrams to the surveys. (i)** _____ **(ii)** _____ **(iii)** _____

b   **How would you describe the relationship between height and weight?**

_____

c   **How would you describe the relationship shown in (i)?**

_____

d   **Graph (iii) shows a negative correlation. What does this mean?**

_____

PAGE TOTAL

Test 9	Time started	:
	Time finished	:

Significant figures

1 Round off the following to the number of significant figures shown:

a 8495 = _____ (to 2 sig fig)

b 2978 = _____ (to 2 sig fig)

c 6.38125 = _____ (to 3 sig fig)

d 0.10307 = _____ (to 3 sig fig)

Squares, square roots and cubes

2 Match the sums to the answers. One has been done for you.

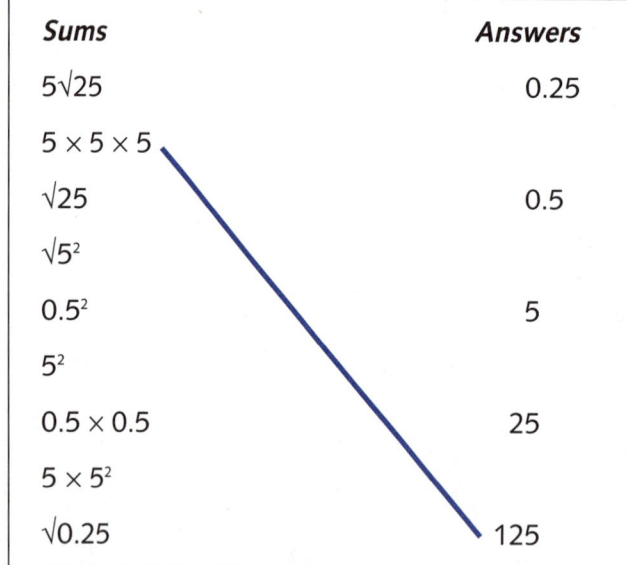

Sums	Answers
$5\sqrt{25}$	0.25
$5 \times 5 \times 5$	
$\sqrt{25}$	0.5
$\sqrt{5^2}$	
0.5^2	5
5^2	
0.5×0.5	25
5×5^2	
$\sqrt{0.25}$	125

Finding the nth term

3 Find the next term and the *n*th term of the following sequences:

a 2 6 12 20 30 ____   *n*th term = _____

b 2 8 18 32 50 ____   *n*th term = _____

c 3 9 19 33 51 ____   *n*th term = _____

PAGE TOTAL

Inequalities

4 The inequality $-1 < x \leq 5$ is shown like this on a number line:

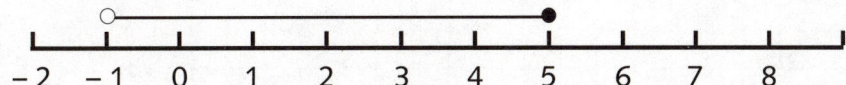

Write down the inequalities shown on each of these number lines:

a 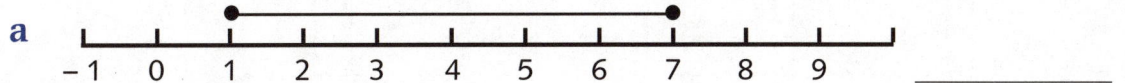 _____ ☐

b 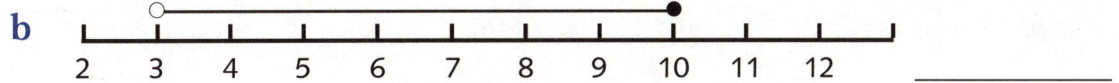 _____ ☐

c _____ ☐

Using a graph to solve simultaneous equations

5

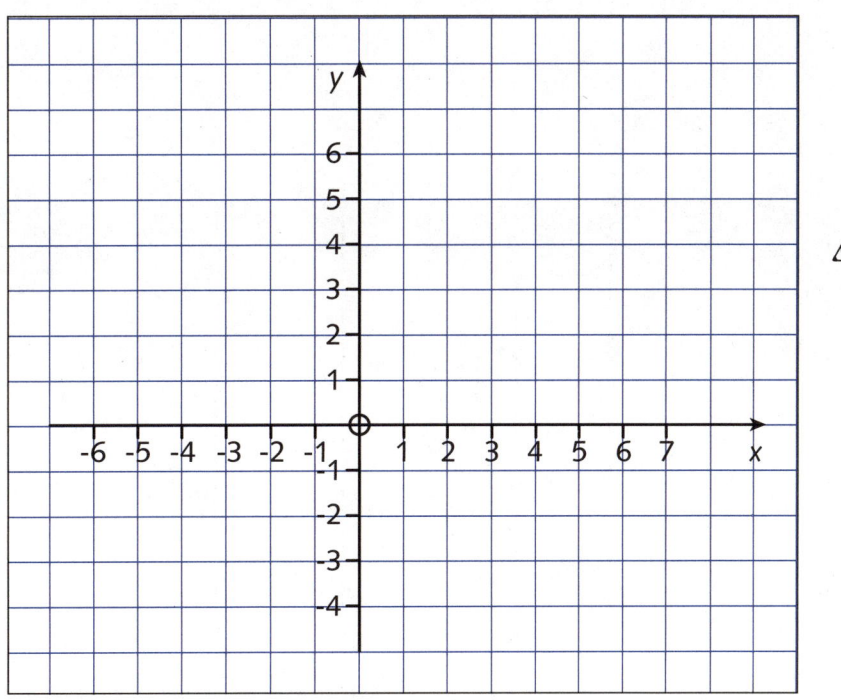

a Plot the line $y = 2x + 3$ on the graph.

b Plot the line $x + y = 6$ on the graph.

c Use the graph to solve the equations $y = 2x + 3$ and $x + y = 6$.

$x =$ _____ and $y =$ _____

PAGE TOTAL

Loci

6

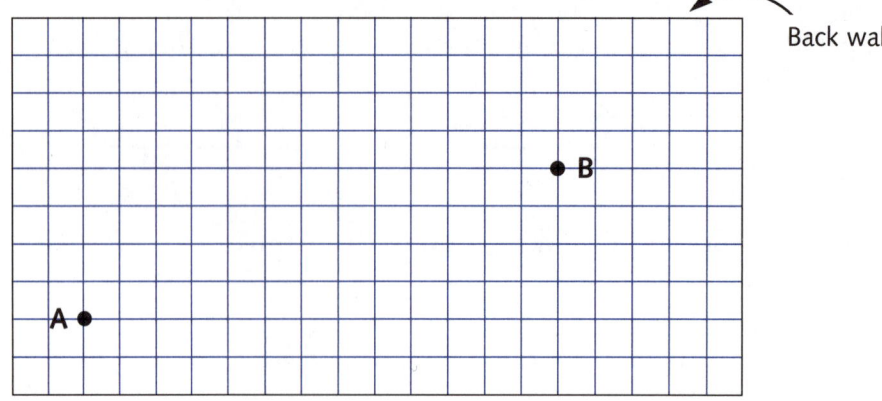

Back wall

a   A gardener wants to build a path so that it is equidistant from the two trees A and B. Draw the path on the plan.

b   Plot another path so that it is always 2 metres from the back wall. Each square in the plan represents one square metre on the ground.

Volume

7   Calculate the volume of each of these containers to the nearest cm³:

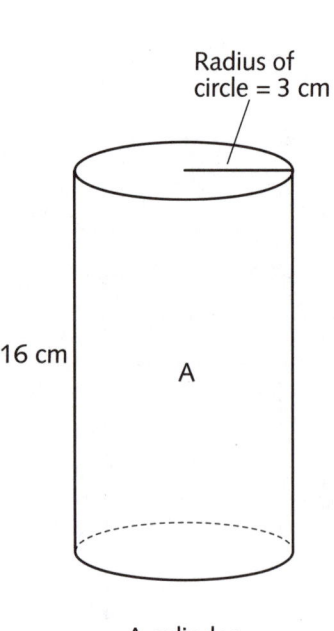

Radius of circle = 3 cm

16 cm

A

A cylinder

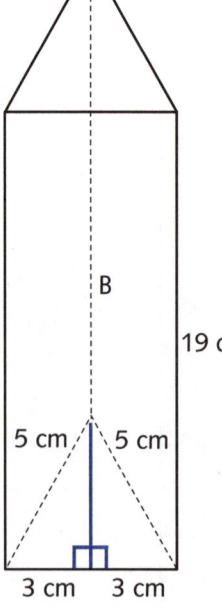

B

19 cm

5 cm   5 cm

3 cm   3 cm

A triangular prism

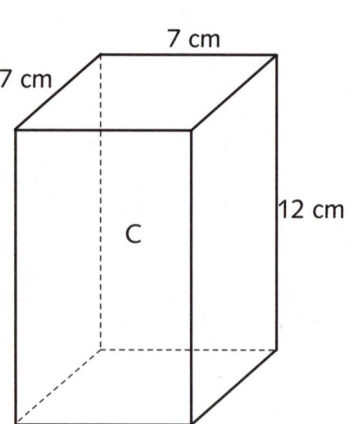

7 cm

7 cm

C

12 cm

A cuboid

A = _____

B = _____

C = _____

PAGE TOTAL

Designing questionnaires, line of best fit

8 **a** Yasmin and Harry are designing a questionnaire to find out whether people who play computer games watch less television. These are their questions:

i) How long do you spend watching television each day?
ii) Which do you like better – computer games or television?

Rewrite their questions to give more precise data.

i) _____

ii) _____

b Yasmin and Harry planned to use all the members of their families as a sample. What is wrong with this sample?

_____

c Which of these would make the best sample:
i) all the students in their class,
ii) 6 students from each of 5 year groups,
iii) a random selection of 20 students from their school?

_____

d Harry and Yasmin plot their data on a scattergram. Estimate and draw in the line of best fit.

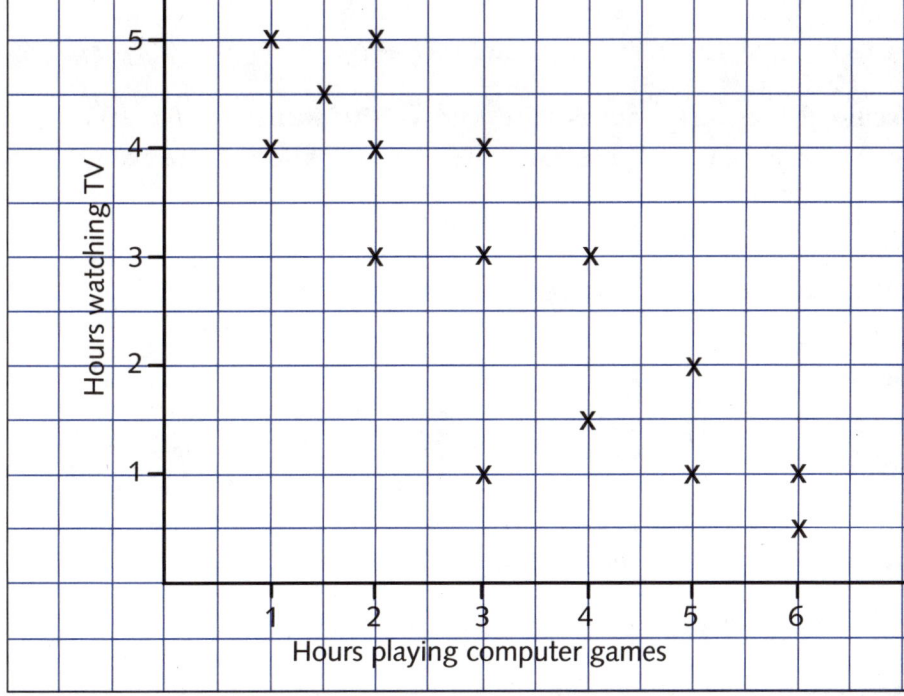

e Use the line of best fit to predict how long someone who watches television for 3 hours is likely to spend playing computer games.

PAGE TOTAL

• Test 10 •

Time started [:   ]
Time finished [:   ]

Estimating calculations

1 Estimate the following calculations by first rounding off appropriately:

a $\dfrac{58.94 \times 24.31}{64.81}$

≈ _____

b $\dfrac{9.06 + 8.793 - 2.541}{(2.64 + 1.8)}$

≈ _____

c $\dfrac{0.07 \times 1.81}{0.1904}$

≈ _____

d $\dfrac{0.571(8.32 + 1.75)}{2.61 \times 0.84}$

≈ _____

Ratio

2 Marie is making crumble topping for an apple pie using an old recipe. The recipe requires:

4 oz flour   2 oz margarine   1 oz sugar

a **What is the ratio of flour : margarine : sugar?** _____

b **Marie's scale shows only grams. She knows she wants to use 200 g of flour. How many grams of margarine and sugar should she weigh out?**

   Margarine _____ g   **Sugar** _____ g

Dave is making a cake from the same book. His recipe says he needs:

12 oz flour   6 oz sugar   4 oz margarine   4 eggs

c **What is the simplest ratio of flour : sugar : margarine ?** _____

d **Dave discovers he has only 3 eggs. How many ounces of flour, sugar and margarine should he use to keep the ingredients in the right proportion?**

   Flour _____   **Sugar** _____   **Margarine** _____

PAGE
TOTAL

Solving inequalities

3 Solve the following inequalities:

a $x + 2 \leq 3x - 12$ _____ ☐

b $6 + 3x > 5x - 12$ _____ ☐

c $x^2 - 3x \geq 2x + 25 - 5x$ _____ ☐

d $12 > 6 + \dfrac{3x}{2}$ _____ ☐

Solving simultaneous equations algebraically

4 Solve the following simultaneous equations algebraically:

a $3x + 2y = 7$
       $x - 5y = 8$

b $5x + 2y = 0$
       $-2x + y = 9$

$x =$ _____ and $y =$ _____ $x =$ _____ and $y =$ _____   ☐☐ ☐☐

c $3x - 2y = 5$
       $5x + 4y = 12$

d $4x + y = -2$
       $y - 2x = 7$

$x =$ _____ and $y =$ _____ $x =$ _____ and $y =$ _____   ☐☐ ☐☐

Pythagoras' theorem, composite areas

5 Students are decorating the school hall for a Christmas dance. They decide to hang two streamers as shown on this plan:

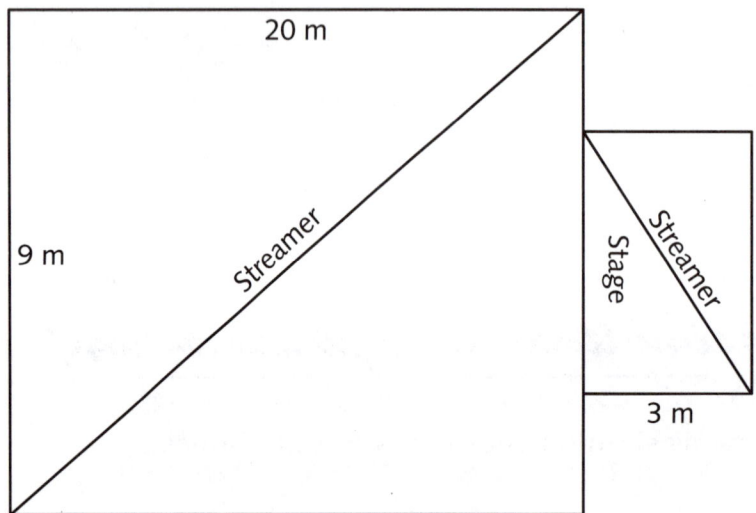

a Calculate the length of streamer needed for the hall to the nearest metre:

_____

They worked out that they needed 5 metres for the stage.

b Calculate the width of the stage: _____

Imran has designed a special area of the floor to be marked out for dancing.

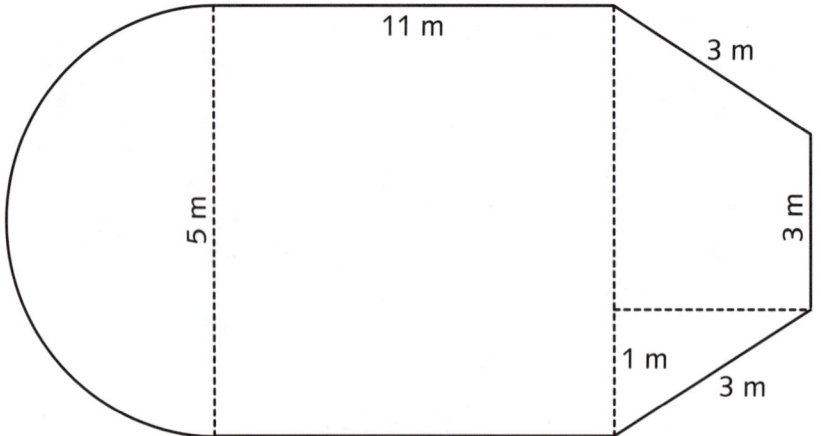

c What is the area of the dance floor to the nearest square metre?

_____

d What area is left for tables and chairs? _____

PAGE TOTAL

Handling group data

6 The students in classes 9D and 9S scored the following marks in a test:

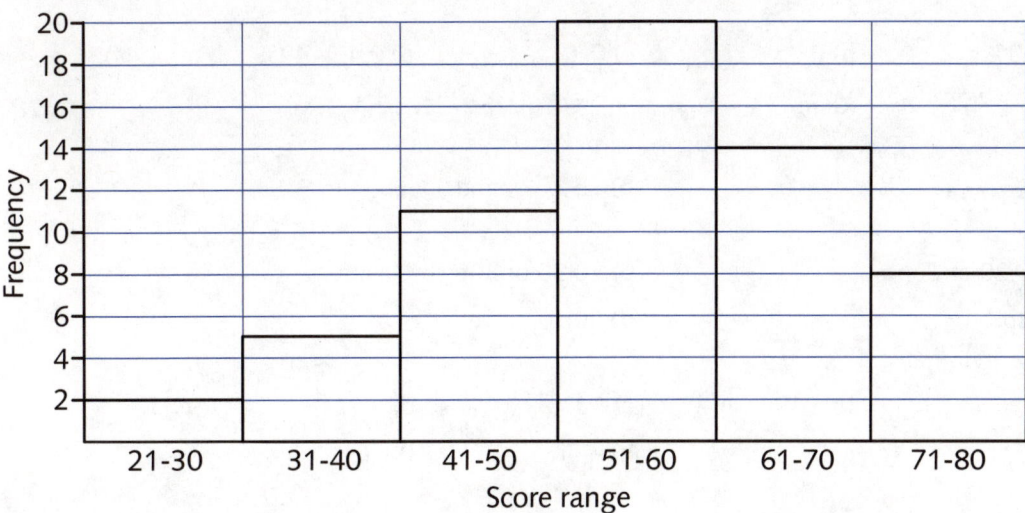

a What is the modal group of scores? _____

b Complete this table and use it to help you estimate the mean score:

Score range	Frequency (f)	Midpoint (x)	fx
21 – 30	2	25.5	51
31 – 40	5		
41 – 50			
51 – 60			
61 – 70			
71 – 80			

Mean score: _____

c What is the probability that a student picked at random scored 61–70?

_____

d What is the probability that a student picked at random scored 51–60?

_____

e What is the probability that a student picked at random scored over 50?

_____

PAGE
TOTAL

• Answers to Test 1 with *Hints* •

1 a) .01   **b)** 5074.21   **c)** 72.54

2 a) 20%   **b)** 0.25   **c)** 0.3; $\frac{3}{10}$ **d)** 0.4;   40%   **e)** $\frac{3}{5}$; 60%

   f) $\frac{3}{4}$;   75%   **g)** $\frac{9}{10}$

3 a) $\frac{24}{60} = \frac{4}{10} = 40\%$ **b)** 25% = $\frac{1}{4}$ and $\frac{1}{4} \times 60 = 15$

4 a) £0.20 or 20p   **b)** £0.30 or 30p

   c) 12p   **d)** 30p

5 a) 0   **b)** – 19   **c)** 10   **d)** – 12   **e)** 32

   f) – 5   **g)** 9   **h)** – 5   **i)** – 6

6 a) 48 kg   **b)** 106 lb   **c)** 7 st 8 lb

7 a) HH, HT, TH, TT   **b)** $\frac{1}{4}$ **c)** $\frac{1}{2}$

8 Angle of shaded sector = 65°

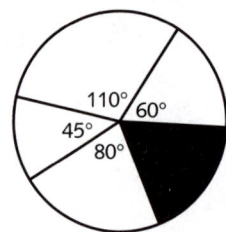

9

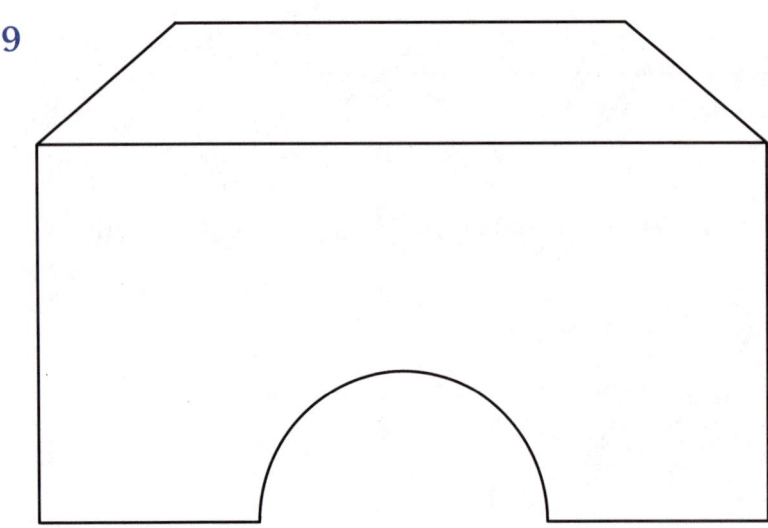

• Answers to Test 2 •

1 6   2.4   9.6
   120   2
   48   3   2400

2 **a)** – 1, 9   **b)** 1.89, 1.95   **c)** 1.2, – 0.4
Three possible answers are:
   d) 1 4 7 10   The rule is add three to the last number.
   e) 1 4 9 16   The rule is the next square number.
   f) 1 4 16 64   The rule is multiply the last number by 4.

3 **a)** £15   **b)** £2   **c)** No   **d)** audio tape, jeans and T-shirt
   e) £3   **f)** 50%   **g)** £16   **h)** $\frac{1}{5}$

4 **a)** 8 cm   **b)** 18 sq cm   **c)**

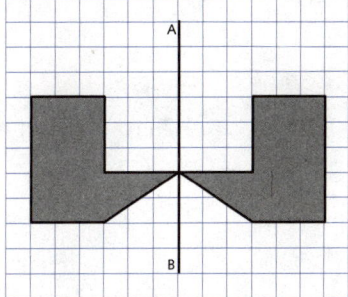

5 **a)** Net a) is correct.   **b)** This is one possible answer:

6 **a)** Total: 76   150   111   **b)** Crisps   **c)** 23

   d)

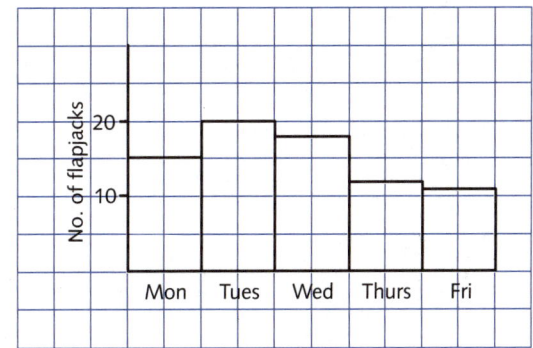

7 **a)** 18   **b)** There are only 4 blue and white cars but 5 yellow and green cars.
   c) $\frac{2}{18} = \frac{1}{9}$ **d)** yellow   **e)** red

TOTAL MARKS FOR TEST 2 = 50
25 or less = Lots to do!   26 to 34 = Revise your weak spots...   35+ = You should achieve level 4

• Answers to Test 3 •

1 a) 630   **b)** 8100   **c)** 810   **d)** 630   **e)** 63   **f)** 8100

Boxes a) and d) are equal; and boxes b) and f) are equal.

2

Simple fraction	Decimal	Percentage
$\frac{1}{10}$	0.1	10%
$\frac{1}{4}$	0.25	25%
$\frac{2}{5}$	0.4	40%
$\frac{1}{2}$	0.5	50%
$\frac{3}{5}$	0.6	60%
$\frac{7}{10}$	0.7	70%
$\frac{3}{4}$	0.75	75%
$\frac{4}{5}$	0.8	80%

3 a) £1.78   **b)** £0.22 or 22p   **c)** £5.93   **d)** £4.07   **e)** £3.75

f) a felt-tip pen   **g)** six   **h)** two

4 a) A and C are congruent; B and F are congruent.

b) 245 mm or 24.5 cm   **c)** 2310 + 777 mm² = 3087 mm² or 30.87 cm²

5 a) $\frac{1}{6}$ **b)** $\frac{2}{6} = \frac{1}{3}$ **c)** $\frac{2}{3}$ **d)** 0   **e)** 1

6 a) 153 cm   **b)** 148 cm   **d)** 152–153 cm   **e)** 150–151 cm

Height (cm)	Tally	Frequency
148-149	卌 l	6
150-151	卌 llll	9
152-153	卌	5
154-155	ll	2
156-157	lll	3

f)

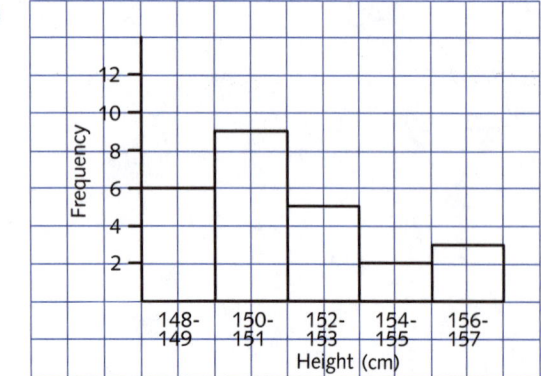

TOTAL MARKS FOR TEST 3 = 50
25 or less = Lots to do!   26 to 34 = Revise your weak spots...   35+ = You should achieve level 4

• 54 •

• **Answers to Test 4** •

1 a) 4°C   **b)** – 1°C

   c) Range for week 2 is 12 degrees.   **d)** Range for week 1 is 15 degrees.

   e) Mean for week 2 is 4°C.   **f)** Mean for week 1 is –1°C.

   g) Week 2 is warmer, and the temperature is less variable than in week 1.

2 estimate: **a)** 20,000   **b)** 32,000   **c)** 27,000   **d)** 800,000
    exact answer: **a)** 22,274   **b)** 30,888   **c)** 25,396   **d)** 779,145

    estimate: **e)** 5   **f)** 40   **g)** 140   **h)** 100
    exact answer: **e)** 4.4875   **f)** 37.3125   **g)** 140.4375   **h)** 108.8

    (There are many ways of approximating, so your estimates may differ.)

3 a) 17   **b)** – 40   **c)** $3n - 7$ **d)** $T = £38$ **e)** $T = £31.40$

4 a) A is (3, 6)   **b)** B is (–8, 3)   **c)** C is (–6, –4)   **d)** D is (6, –5)

   e)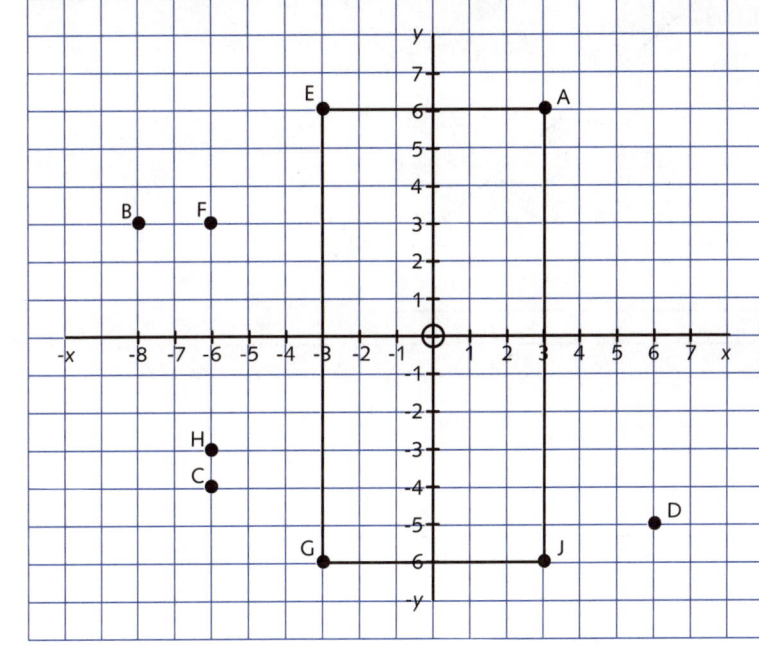

   f) AEGJ is a rectangle.   **g)** Perimeter of AEGJ is 36.

   h) Area is 72.   **i)** F, H and C are in a straight line.

5 a) 27 cm   **b)** 276 mm   **c)** 10.48 in   **d)** 31.5 cm
   e) 2500 g   **f)** 126.5 lb

6 a) 8   **b)** 6   **c)** 8   **d)** 2

TOTAL MARKS FOR TEST 4 = 50
25 or less = Lots to do!   26 to 34 = Revise your weak spots...   35+ = You should achieve level 5

• Answers to Test 5 •

1 a) ÷ 100; × 1000   **b)** 0.86; ÷ 1000; 0.00086   **c)** ÷ 100; 0.034; × 10,000

2 a)

	Sun	Mon	Tues	Wed	Thurs	Fri	Sat
Hire charge	£22.40	£22.40	£22.40	£22.40	£22.40	£22.40	£22.40
Miles/day	64.6	81.2	91.8	124.2	80.6	55.0	150.5
Mileage charge (to nearest p)	£5.17	£6.50	£7.34	£9.94	£6.45	£4.40	£12.04
Total charge	£27.57	£28.90	£29.74	£32.34	£28.85	£26.80	£34.44

b) £208.64

c) $C = h + 0.08m$ where C = daily cost, h = hire charge, and m = number of miles per day.
In *this* case, $C = 22.40 + 0.08m$

3
  a) $n = 4$;   **b)** $n = 5$;   **c)** $n = 5$ **d)** $n = 2$

4

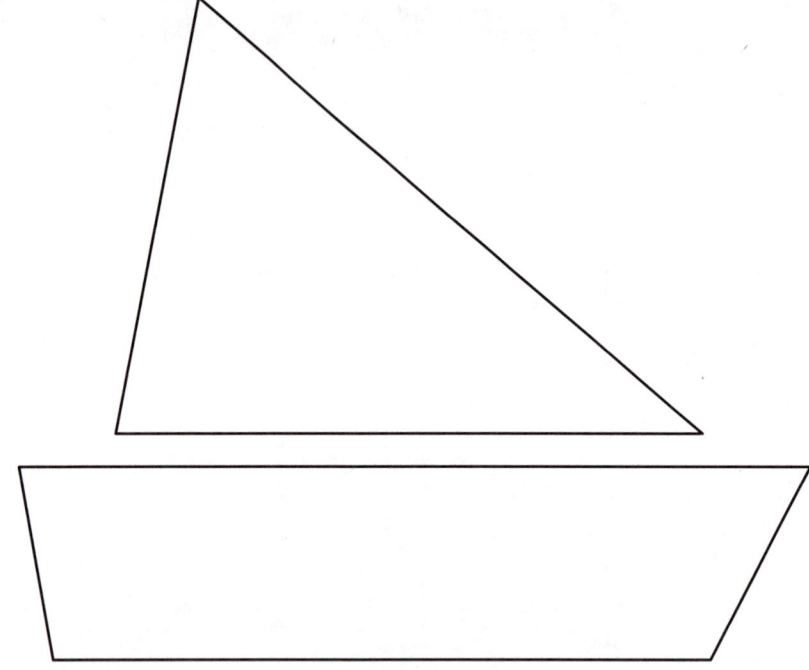

5
  a) July and August   **b)** 200 hours   **c)** May
  d) Range is 150 hours   **e)** Total is 2050 hours   **f)** Mean is $170\frac{5}{6}$ hours

6
  a) $\frac{26}{52} = \frac{1}{2}$ **b)** $\frac{13}{52} = \frac{1}{4}$ **c)** $\frac{1}{52}$ **d)** $\frac{12}{52} = \frac{3}{13}$

7
  a) Shapes B, C, D, E, F and G   **b)** Shapes C and G
  c) Shapes D and F   **d)** Any shape which has no lines of symmetry
  e) H, I, N, O, S, X, Z

TOTAL MARKS FOR TEST 5 = 50
25 or less = Lots to do!   26 to 34 = Revise your weak spots...   35+ = You should achieve level 5

• Answers to Mental Arithmetic •

Test A (Lower tier levels 3–5)

1 2540
2 Either 35.1, 35.2, 35.3 or 35.4
3 $m = -5$
4 £1.80
5 90 tins
6 16 cats and dogs
7 £15
8 -30
9 60°
10 25 sq cm
11 a triangular prism
12 3.50 (ten to four)
13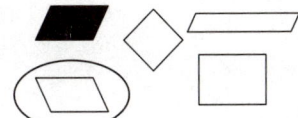

Test B (Lower tier levels 3–5)

1 8
2 3000 g
3 90° (a right angle)
4 $p = 4$
5 20
6 ◐
7 £3.01
8 13
9 four
10 0.75 metres
11 81
12 a circle
13 two lines of symmetry

Test C (Higher tier levels 6–7)

1 0.0672
2
3 4.5
4 $m = 5$
5 70°
6 15 sq m
7 0.125
8 140 minutes
9 36
10 9 nights
11 £80
12 5 cm
13 13,695

Test D (Higher tier levels 6–7)

1 0.56 km
2 5 cm
3 £1.50
4
5 $\frac{1}{2}$
6 2
7 7
8 16
9 27p
10 420 km
11 $\frac{10}{13}$
12 4 cm
13 60

TOTAL MARKS FOR EACH MENTAL ARITHMETIC TEST = 13
Lower Tier: 5 or less = level 3   5 to 10 = level 4   10+ = level 5
Higher Tier: 5 or less = Lots to do!   5 to 10 = level 6   10+ = level 7

• Answers to Test 6 with *Hints* •

1 a) 32   **b)** 70   **c)** 45   **d)** 20.3   **e)** 0.9
  f) 0.4   **g)** $\frac{1}{3}$ **h)** $\frac{2}{5}$

2 a) 0.28 metres   **b)** 0.65 metres   **c)** 0.52 metres   **d)** 4.78 metres

3 a) $3x - y$ **b)** $5m - 4n$ **c)** $4a + 5b$ **d)** $s + 2w$

4 a) $7n - 2$ **b)** $6n + 6$ **c)** $n = 8$

5 £14.70

6 a) 3.6 hours   **b)** 3.5 hours   **c)** 450 km   **d)** 5.5 kg

7 a) red 11 litres   yellow 44 litres   white 22 litres
  b) red 15 litres   blue 75 litres   yellow 60 litres   white 30 litres

8

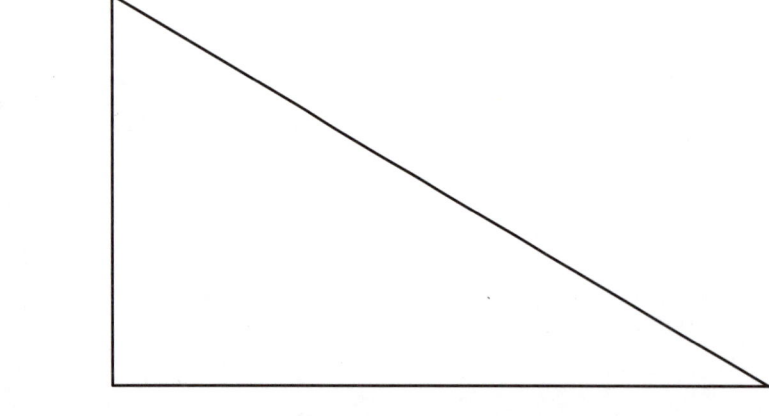

9 a) $\frac{1}{36}$ **b)** $\frac{2}{36} = \frac{1}{18}$ **c)** $\frac{10}{36} = \frac{5}{18}$

• Answers to Test 7 •

1 **a)** 20   **b)** 40%   **c)** 60   **d)** 25%   **e)** 10%

   f) 40   **g)** 20   **h)** 62.5%

2 **a)** 19   **b)** nth term is $3n + 1$ **c)** 35   **d)** nth term is $n^2 - 1$

   e) − 1   1   3   5

3 **a)** $x = 4$ **b)** $x = 3$ **c)** $a - c = 12$ or $a = c + 12$ **d)** $(a - 2) = 2(c + 2)$

   e) Ali started with 18 cards and Lisa started with 6 cards.

4 **a)**

x	$5x - 3$
1	2
2	7
3	12
4	17
5	22

b)

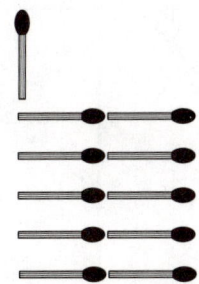

c) nth term = $2n + 1$

5 **a)** 3225 cm³   **b)** 273,600 cm³   **c)** 84 packets   (Remember – you have to round down here.)

6 **a)** 60°   **b)** Opposite angle to 60°   **c)** 120°

   d) It's a complementary angle to BAD. (There are other possible answers too.)

   e) ABC is an equilateral triangle (all angles equal).   **f)** Area = $\frac{1}{2}$ (6 x 5.2) = 15.6 sq cm

   g) ABED is a trapezium.   **h)** Area = $\frac{1}{2}$ (6 + 3) x 2.6 = 11.7 sq cm

7 **a)** 36   **b)** 25%   **c)** 16.6%   **d)** $\frac{3}{36} = \frac{1}{12}$

   e) $\frac{12}{36} = \frac{1}{3}$ **f)** $1 - \frac{8}{36} = \frac{7}{9}$ **g)** $\frac{6}{24} = \frac{1}{4}$ **h)** $\frac{12}{24} = \frac{1}{2}$

   i)

Number of beans		Angle in pie chart
Orange	2	$\frac{2}{24} = 30°$
Yellow	9	$\frac{9}{24} = 135°$
Green	4	$\frac{4}{24} = 60°$
Blue	3	$\frac{3}{24} = 45°$
Brown	6	$\frac{6}{24} = 90°$

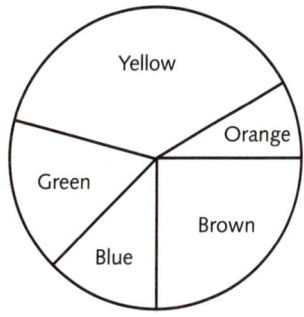

• Answers to Test 8 •

1 a) Alex £25   Sophie £20   Darren £15   **b)** £30   **c)** £18

   d) £18   **e)** Sophie (£38)

2 a) 4.47   **b)** 2385.56   **c)** 10.07   **d)** 7.90   **e)** 8.66

3 a) $5a + 2b$ **b)** $s + 7t - 6$ **c)** $5x - 11y + 4$

4 a)

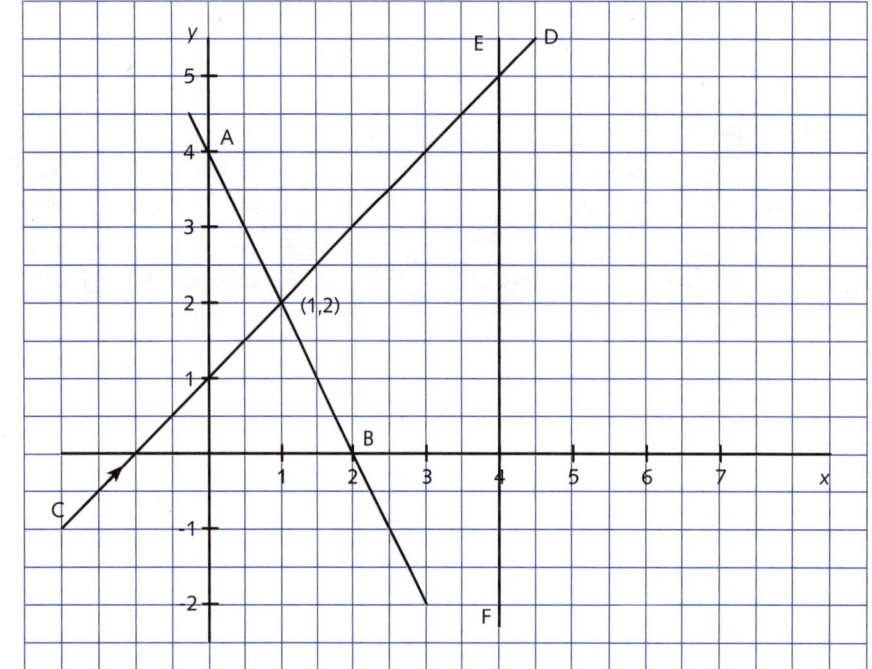

   b) point (4, 5)   **c)** point (1, 2)   **d)** EF is $x = 4$ **e)** $y = x + 1$

5 a) 80 cm   **b)** 62.8 cm   **c)** 502.4 cm   **d)** 8 times   **e)** 20,096 cm²

6 a) 180   **b)** 15 km on bearing 090   **c)** 115   **d)** 222

7 a)   **b)** $\frac{1}{4}$ **c)** $\frac{1}{2}$

	First coin	
Second coin	HH	TH
	HT	TT

8 a) (i) B   **(ii)** A   **(iii)** C

   b) There is a positive correlation between height and weight.

   c) There is no relationship between month of birth and distance of home from school.

   d) The more hours a student watches television the less he or she spends doing homework.

TOTAL MARKS FOR TEST 8 = 50
25 or less = Lots to do!   26 to 34 = Revise your weak spots...   35+ = You should achieve level 6

• Answers to Test 9 •

1 a) 8500   **b)** 3000   **c)** 6.38   **d)** 0.103

2
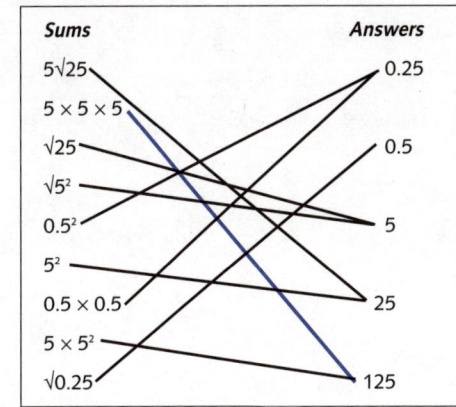

3 a) 42; nth term $= n^2 + n$, or $n(n + 1)$ **c)** 73; nth term $= 2n^2 + 1$
   b) 72; nth term $= n \times 2n$, or $2n^2$

4 a) $1 \leq x \leq 7$ **b)** $3 < x \leq 10$ **c)** $-3 \leq x < 2$

5 a & b)
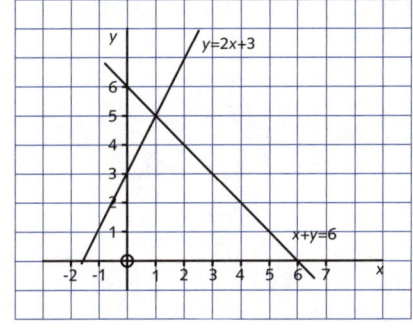

6
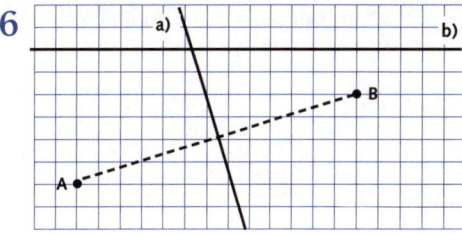

c) $x = 1$ and $y = 5$

7 A = 452 cm³   **B** = 228 cm³   **C** = 588 cm³

8 a) Questions need to be precise and limited. For example: i) Approximately how long do you usually
   watch TV each day: a) 1 hour   b) 2 hours   c) 3 hours   d) 4 hours   e) 5 hours   f) 6 hours or more
   ii) Approximately how long do you usually spend playing computer games per day: a) 1 hour
   b) 2 hours   c) 3 hours   d) 4 hours   e) 5 hours   f) 6 hours or more
   b) Most adults and children under 5 do not play computer games and a single family would give
   a biased result.
   c) ii)   **d)**   **e)** 3 hours

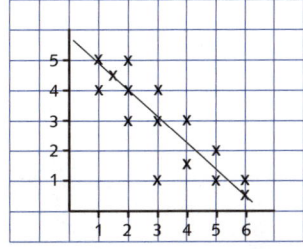

TOTAL MARKS FOR TEST 9 = 40
20 or less = Lots to do!   21 to 27 = Revise your weak spots...   28+ = You should achieve level 7

• 61 •

• Answers to Test 10 •

1 a) $60 \times 20 \div 60 \approx 20$ **b)** $(9 + 9 - 3) \div (3 + 2) \approx 3$

  c) $0.07 \times 2 \div 0.2 \approx 0.7$ **d)** $0.6(8 + 2) \div (3 \times 0.8) \approx 6 \div 2.4 \approx 3$

  (There are many ways of approximating, so your answers may differ.)

2 a) $4 : 2 : 1$ **b)** Margarine 100 g   Sugar 50 g   **c)** $12 : 6 : 4 = 6 : 3 : 2$

  d) Flour 9 oz   Sugar 4.5 oz   Margarine 3 oz

3 a) $x \geq 7$ **b)** $x < 9$ **c)** $x \geq 5$ and $x \leq -5$ **d)** $x < 4$

4 a) $x = 3;\ y = -1$ **b)** $x = -2;\ y = 5$

  c) $x = 2;\ y = \frac{1}{2}$ **d)** $x = -1\frac{1}{2};\ y = 4$

5 a) 22 metres   **b)** 4 metres   **c)** 76 sq m   **d)** 104 sq m

6 a) 51–60

b)

Score range	Frequency (f)	Midpoint (x)	fx
21 – 30	2	25.5	51
31 – 40	5	35.5	177.5
41 – 50	11	45.5	500.5
51 – 60	20	55.5	1110
61 – 70	14	65.5	917
71 – 80	8	75.5	604

Mean score 56

  c) $\frac{14}{60} = \frac{7}{30}$ **d)** $\frac{1}{3}$ **e)** $\frac{42}{60} = \frac{7}{10}$

TOTAL MARKS FOR TEST 10 = 40
20 or less = Lots to do!   21 to 27 = Revise your weak spots...   28+ = You should achieve level 7

• 62 •

• Revision Index •

This chart shows the main topics in the National Curriculum that are tested at Key Stage 3. The numbers in each row refer to question numbers. Tick each question as you complete the tests and use the chart to:

1 identify your strengths and weaknesses
2 plan your revision ✓
3 find the topics you want.

Topic in curriculum	Levels 4–6 Test 1	Level 4 Test 2	Level 4 Test 3	Level 5 Test 4	Level 5 Test 5	Levels 6–7 Test 6	Level 6 Test 7	Level 6 Test 8	Level 7 Test 9	Level 7 Test 10
NUMBER										
Approximating				2				2		1
Decimals	1 2	1	2		1	1				
Fractions as parts	2	1	2			1				
Money calculations	4	3	3		2					
Multiplication and division		1	1		1					
Negative numbers	5			1						
Number lines		2								
Percentages	2 3 4	1 3	2				1 7			
Ratio & proportion						5 6 7		1		2
Significant figures									1	
Squares, square roots						1 2		2	2	
ALGEBRA										
Formulae/substitution				3	2					
Inequalities									4	3
Number pattern & finding the *n*th term		2					2 4		3	
Plotting points and lines on a graph				4				4	5 6	
Simplifying						3 4		3		
Solving simple equations					3	4	3			
Solving simultaneous equations									5	4

• Revision Index •

Topic in curriculum	Levels 4–6 Test 1	Level 4 Test 2	Level 4 Test 3	Level 5 Test 4	Level 5 Test 5	Levels 6–7 Test 6	Level 6 Test 7	Level 6 Test 8	Level 7 Test 9	Level 7 Test 10
SHAPE, SPACE AND MEASUREMENT										
Accurate drawing	8 9				4	8		*		
Area		4	4	4		2	6	5		5
Bearings								6		
Circumference/perimeter		4	4	4		2		5		
Congruency			4							
Geometry/angles	8						6			
Metric and imperial units	6			5						
Nets of solid shapes		5								
Pythagoras' theorem										5
Reading scales	6		6	1						
Symmetry					7					
Transformations		4								
Volume							5		7	
HANDLING DATA										
Bar charts/frequency charts		6	6		5		7			6
Grouped data			6							6
Mean and range				1	5					6
Mode and median		6	6		5					6
Pie charts				6			7			
Probability	7	7	5		6	9	7	7		6
Questionnaires									8	
Scattergrams								8	8	